D0982433

Reverence for Life

ALBERT SCHWEITZER

Reverence for Life

Translated by Reginald H. Fuller

THE PILGRIM PRESS
New York City

Reverence for Life. Copyright © 1969 by Rhena Eckert-Schweitzer.

Reprinted by arrangement with Harper & Row, Publishers, Inc., and Irvington Publishers, Inc. All rights reserved.

Reverence for Life was originally published in German under the title, *Strassburger Predigten,* copyright © 1966 by C.H. Beck'sche Verlagsbuch-handlung (Oscar Beck), München.

Library of Congress Cataloging in Publication Data

Schweitzer, Albert, 1875-1965.
    Reverence for life.

    Translation of Strassburger Predigten.
    Reprint of the 1st ed. published by Harper & Row,
New York.
    1. Sermons, English—Translations from German.
2. Sermons, German—Translations into English. I. Title.
BV4254.G3S3213 1979   252′.04   79-19338
ISBN 0-89197-920-4 (Irvington)
ISBN 0-8298-0384-X (Pilgrim)

Printed in The United States of America.

Contents

Foreword by D. Elton Trueblood   7

1   Creative Suffering   13

2   We Shall Be Exalted   20

3   The Courage of Action   24

4   Christ in Our Life   30

5   Gratitude—the Secret of Life   36

6   Compelling Hope   43

7   The Call to Mission   50

8   The Life of Service   58

9   Overcoming Death   67

10   My Brother's Keeper   77

11   Be True to Yourself   82

12   The Peace of God   88

13   The Future of Mankind   95

14   Sacrifice of Others   101

15   Reverence for Life   108

16   Ethics of Compassion   118

17   Fulfill Your Destiny   127

Editor's Postscript: Albert Schweitzer as Preacher
by Ulrich Neuenschwander   143

Foreword

AT THE HEIGHT of his influence Albert Schweitzer was often referred to as the most famous of living men. He inspired millions by his revelation of how rich a human life can be. But while Schweitzer has been an inspiration, particularly in his many-sidedness, he has also been an enigma. He expressed himself freely in his philosophical and theological works, and he published several autobiographical volumes, but, though these were widely appreciated, many readers have expressed deep misgivings about the soundness of the great man's ideas. Now, at last, by the publication of some of his sermons, we have a revelation of certain sides of a remarkable life of which we were formerly unaware.

Personally, I am grateful to those who have made this new publication possible. My own excited interest in Schweitzer's life and thought goes back to 1924 when I first encountered, in the volume *On the Edge of the Primeval Forest,* the moving idea of the "fellowship of those who bear the mark of pain." Later, in 1930, I had some correspondence with Schweitzer when, as a graduate student, I thought that I might write a dissertation on his moral philosophy. Though he graciously gave permission to proceed, I decided, for a variety of reasons, not to do so, but my interest in his thinking never ended. I was not sure at that time that he was a great philosopher, but I could never doubt that his life was dominated by the person of Jesus Christ. And always there was the helpful observation that, just as the original disciples followed Christ before they realized fully who he was, we too may follow before we have all of the answers, and may likewise be provided our revelation only after having been His followers.

Though I was well aware that Albert Schweitzer preached a great deal both before and after he became a physician, I never encountered any of his sermons until I was privileged to read the present collection prior to publication. What I find in this increases my sense of wonder, though it does not increase my surprise. It pleases me to find that, like other speakers and writers, the famous missionary doctor preached many of his ideas before they were cast into essay form, thus following the experimental method. We now know that this was particularly true of the conception of "Reverence for Life," which provides this collection with its title. We knew earlier how the basic idea was conceived, but now we also know that it was preached to fellow worshipers.

On the whole the sermons seem contemporary. It is hard for me to believe that when I was a small child Albert Schweitzer was already giving expression to thoughts which still seem fresh. Very early in the twentieth century, he understood that Christianity is not a merely spiritual religion and that the popular arguments against missions are superficial ones. Years before our cult of irrationality had become really popular, Schweitzer saw its serious dangers.

What pleases me most about the new publication is its revelation of the author's deep personal piety. This is especially important today when so many suppose that it is necessary to choose between the cultivation of the inner life and involvement in social action. The world has long been aware of the famous doctor's human service, especially in his medical work in Africa, but now we can ascertain better than was possible heretofore the personal piety out of which the service arose. It is now obvious that the widely recognized sensitivity to human suffering did not stand alone and rootless, but emerged from hours and days of disciplined meditation. The great truth is that Schweitzer's outer life depended upon his inner rootedness! We shall long debate his orthodoxy, but we cannot deny his closeness to Christ.

D. ELTON TRUEBLOOD

Reverence for Life

{ 1 }

*Creative Suffering**

Blessed are they that mourn: for they shall be comforted.

MATTHEW 5:4

TODAY we explore the Beatitudes with which the Lord began the Sermon on the Mount. Last Sunday we talked about the meaning of the remarkable first Beatitude: "Blessed are the poor in spirit, for theirs is the kingdom of God." As we noted then, "poor in spirit" does not mean mentally backward. The poor in spirit are those who consider themselves poor in spiritual blessings, whose hearts are yearning for higher and more precious things.

The Beatitude on which we base today's meditation turns now from the spiritual to the earthly.

What a wonderful thing this is about Jesus: he does not concern himself exclusively with our spiritual being; he can also deal sensitively on a human basis with his fellow men. Have you never noticed when you said the Lord's Prayer that the practical petition for daily bread, our daily needs, comes in the middle of the petitions for spiritual

* *Preached Sunday, May 14, 1900, at the afternoon service at St. Nicolai's Church.*

13

blessings? Jesus didn't tack it on the end as an after-thought. He shares the feelings we have as men concerned with earthly things. This empathy gripped Jesus right at the beginning of the Sermon on the Mount. The people came to him to hear his teaching. As he started his teaching he saw eyes red from weeping and sensed hearts pressed down by the cares of daily life. Jesus was moved by com-passion. Before he continued to speak he wanted to com-fort them, to free their hearts from earthly cares before tell-ing them of heavenly things.

What does this mean, Blessed are those who suffer? "Blessed" has connotations of the dead who have finished their earthly course and are now in their heavenly home, free from all suffering. But that is not what the Lord meant here. Christianity has been reproached for trying to deceive people about the reality of earthly suffering by comforting them with the prospect of the heavenly blessedness await-ing them. Jesus was not thinking of vague future bliss. For he does not say: Blessed eventually will those be who now suffer. Rather he promises: Blessed are you now, right this minute, while you are suffering.

But how can Jesus possibly look on people in the midst of their earthly life and cares and call them "blessed"? In our first two meditations on the Beatitudes we saw the exact meaning of the word "blessed" on Jesus' lips at the beginning of the Sermon on the Mount: it meant that the blessed belonged to the kingdom of God that he was preaching there and then, that was beginning with him there on earth. The meek, the merciful, the pure in heart, and the peacemakers—they are blessed because they belong to the kingdom of God. So, too, are those who suffer, for they belong to the kingdom of God and are the children of God.

The Jewish people, including perhaps many of Jesus'

hearers, expected that in the distant future the Messiah, the Savior, would appear, the kingdom of God would come, and then all earthly suffering would vanish, and all pain would cease. But now the Savior had appeared. He was sitting among them proclaiming the kingdom of God. So why had earthly suffering not been brought to an end? Jesus, by saying, "Blessed are those who suffer," tried to make them understand that suffering does not cease with the kingdom of God. And so it was. He, the Savior, suffered more than anyone. The passing centuries have shown us that suffering still prevails on earth, and those very ones who confess their faith in the Lord and his kingdom must suffer more than the rest. And yet Jesus says: "Blessed are those who suffer."

This means that he has not eradicated suffering from the earth. But our thinking about suffering is changed by his Beatitude. This is just what our blessedness is.

Since men have been able to think, they have always been faced with the same question: Why must we poor mortals in this world suffer so greatly? Countless books, many of them centuries old, reecho the question: How can God allow men, his creatures, to be so haunted by misfortune? There was no answer to the question that haunts every man in his affliction. So men began to go astray. There is no God, they said. Then they thought deeply. They tried to explain why their suffering was necessary. They tried to make it intelligible, something as essential as the light. Just as the light shines and casts shadows, so there must be in the world light and shadows, joy and sorrow. But when sorrow fell upon them, the wisdom they had worked out for themselves could not stand the test. So they saw in all suffering a trial sent by God. Finally, in deep misfortune, they sensed a punishment from God. Thus they suffered doubly, not only outwardly but also in their consciences. Men had such theories at the time of Jesus. In all suffering they tried to see a punishment from God. The tower of Siloam collapsed and killed many people. That made observers ask: "What had these people done to be the victims of this disaster?" A man was born blind. His associates asked Jesus: "Who sinned, this man or his parents, for the misfortune to strike him?" And Jesus answered, "Neither." Already he had turned men's eyes away from their fixed gaze on the abyss of suffering and misfortune and pointed their sights upward. He wiped the tears from their eyes with simple words: "Blessed are those who suffer."

Only now do we really understand what he meant. He is saying: Don't vex your minds by trying to explain the suffering you have to endure in this life. Don't despair. Don't think that God is punishing you or disciplining you or that he has rejected you. Even in the midst of your suffering you are in his kingdom. You are always his children, and he has his protecting arm around you. Everything comes from God. Don't ask why; don't try to understand. Does a child understand everything his father does? Can he comprehend parental wisdom? No—but he can confidently nestle in his father's arms and feel perfect happiness, even while tears glisten in his eyes, because he is his father's child. Yes, blessed are those who suffer. This saying was also the lodestar of Jesus' life. Explained in this way, it was no sham in his mouth; his whole life bore witness to it. He suffered much but never doubted his Father. And when, in mortal agony, he could not comprehend his Father's will, he submitted. As he had taught us, so he prayed: "Thy will be done." There, in Gethsemane, he finished his inner struggle: "Not my will but thine be done."

I never hear or read these words without being reminded

of an event that brought home to my inmost soul what comfort in tribulation we possess in the word and in the life of our Savior. In July it will be four years since I was asked to preach in a certain parish in the Lower Alsace. I can no longer remember what text I had planned to use. On the previous Thursday the whole region, including the parish where I was to preach, had suffered the worst hailstorm to hit our Alsatian land in living memory. On that Saturday night, as I journeyed by train through the area and saw how the fields had been devastated and everything lost, I felt that the sermon I had prepared just wouldn't do. The people would be coming to church expecting to be comforted by the word of God in their misfortune.

And so I asked myself: What shall I say to them—God sent this calamity to test you or to punish you? I am sure that had I expressed such thoughts then, it would have seemed to me sheer blasphemy. As I mused, I visioned the picture of the Lord at Gethsemane, and preached on the text: "Lord, not as I will but as thou wilt." I showed them how we men cannot understand God's ways. But we can understand through Jesus that in all our suffering we still have a Father in heaven. And I could sense that their hearts were calmed.

I know that you are all as convinced as I that in spite of suffering we need not doubt God's love and faithfulness. We are still heirs of his kingdom and still his children, and so we may rest assured that he will always lift us above misfortune. That is why our Lord says to us: "Blessed are those who suffer, for they shall be comforted."

Jesus does not say what kind of suffering or what kind of comfort. And yet I believe his sympathy is so human that he still has a special comfort for each particular suffering. Suppose he came face to face with a woman who mourned her dear one or he gazed at some poor fellow human being who felt orphaned and lonely. If a bent figure sat at his feet, bowed by the loss of all worldly goods, if among his hearers there was someone looking back with a sad and troubled heart on a life misspent—for each he had a special word of comfort. He would have pointed the mother to God, who has the power to give her again what she has lost. He would have taught the orphaned heart to feel sympathy for others. He would have enabled the impoverished one to go back to work, and to him who grieved over a misspent life he would have given courage to start a new life by telling him the parable of the prodigal son. And if we had approached him, he would have been able to comfort us, too, in the same way. He would say to us: Look back at your life. Were there not many things you regarded as a misfortune at the time? And yet, when you look back, don't you recognize in them the ways of God? Don't you see now that it was only temporary and that good fortune was born out of it, like the sun rising from the morning mists?

And then he would look deep into our eyes, and I believe he might have an even greater comfort to give us. Look back at those hours which passed over your life so calmly and contentedly, he would say. If the whole of your life had been a succession of hours like those, do you know what would have become of you? You would become selfish, hardhearted, lonely, without regard for higher things, for the pure, for God—and you would never have felt blessedness. When did it first dawn on you that we men don't live unto ourselves? When did the blessedness of compassion bring comfort to you? In suffering. Where did your heart come close to those who were so distant and cold to you? In suffering. Where did you catch a glimpse of the higher destiny of your life? In suffering. Where did you feel God was near to you? In suffering.

Where did you first realize the blessedness of having a Father in heaven? In suffering. If he spoke to us like this, we would say to him: Now we know what you mean when you say: "Blessed are those who suffer, for they shall be comforted." Now we will continue calmly on the path of life. Joy and sorrow, sorrow and joy, that is what lies before us. But the sorrow no longer frightens us. For in these times we hear the voice of our heavenly Father within us, calling us to himself and to our higher destiny. And when, in the final hour of suffering, death at last approaches us, we smile at him, and hear our hearts say: Come, death of sleep, come, brother, and lead me away. Take the oar of my frail bark and guide me safely to port. Some may dread you, but you are making me glad. For you are the gateway to my Father's everlasting home.

{ 2 }

*We Shall Be Exalted**

*And I, if I be lifted up from the earth, will draw all men
unto me. This he said, signifying what death he should
die.* JOHN *12:32–33*

EACH YEAR, as Passiontide returns, every serious-minded
Christian comes back to the same question: What does the
death of Jesus really mean? Can we understand how the
suffering and dying of this single man on Golgotha has
redeemed us, whatever age we live in? How did it become
the source of unutterable blessing for all men and all
generations? With the words of the hymn, we say:

> When I this miracle would weigh,
> Would sound its depth, its width survey,
> In silent awe I then adore
> God's wondrous love, its endless store.

Jesus himself veiled the redemptive significance of his
death with mysterious sayings. He once said to the disciples
that his death would be a ransom for many. At the Last

** Preached Sunday, February 23, 1902, at the afternoon service at
St. Nicolai's Church.*

Supper he declared that his blood was shed for many for
the forgiveness of sins. But he was silent about the *why*
and the *how*. Jesus' death remains a mystery to be revered.
He chose to point to it out in the distance, knowing men
would never be able to understand it completely. Out text
is just such a pointer. "When I am lifted," Jesus says, "I
will draw all men unto me." Thus he indicates what manner of death he will die. He not only wanted to tell that
he would bleed to death on the cross; he also was drawing
attention to the deeper meaning of this kind of death.

Upon a hill visible from afar, above a great city with its
busy crowds, Jesus is raised on the cross. In other words,
he hangs there in full view of the whole world. Men are
bound to see him whether they want to or not. Even if
they turn their heads, they are compelled to ponder on
what was happening on Golgotha. They must see that such
an example of infinitely loving sacrifice exists in this cold
world—they may care about it, or mock it, or find that it
strangely moves their inmost hearts, but see it they must.

You will say: If it is only an example, it doesn't really
amount to very much. Many times we admire a noble
person and say to ourselves—and really mean it—here is a
quality we would like to possess. But we lack the strength.
The fine example seems only to embarrass us, to reveal how
far it is beyond our reach. You are right. But is the death
on the cross merely an example? No. He who stands under
the cross, he who looks at Jesus with the inner, spiritual
eye, finds the death of Jesus a source of strength. "When I
am lifted up, I will draw all men unto me." Unto me—
I will exercise an influence over their hearts, Jesus promises. From the cross—my hanging there will wonderfully
affect the hearts of men. I will give them strength and joy
to accomplish things they could never do otherwise. From
my cross shall go forth a renewal of meaning in the world.

How true this saying is! Christianity has brought beauty and greatness to the world, but what true efficacy does it have other than the power of the cross of Christ? Its power has accomplished all of man's work that is great, noble, and holy.

How does this power manifest itself in us? There is serious prophecy in this saying: "When I am lifted up, I will draw all men unto me." The Lord will draw us after him into suffering. And through this sorrow he will draw all of us to himself. Paul the apostle speaks of himself in a time of great tribulation as filling up that which is lacking of the sufferings of Jesus. A beautiful saying. We too must all pass through suffering. We must not tremble or ask questions. We must know that misfortune is part of what it means to be a Christian and that Jesus draws us with him into his suffering.

And why? Because suffering is exaltation. Just as Jesus was exalted on the cross at Golgotha above the world, awaiting the consummation and transfiguration which the heavenly Father would grant him, so we too must suffer in order to be exalted above the world. In pain we discover the existence of something higher than earthly happiness and physical contentment. Then we can gradually detach ourselves from those things which hold our senses captive here below; we set our eyes on the eternal and other-worldly and strive to rise higher and higher. That is why our Lord says: "When I am lifted up, I will draw all men to me." Whatever we suffer and endure, the hand of our Savior grasps us, and his voice says to us: Higher, ever higher.

A woman who was very ill said to her minister: "I have to suffer a lot, and often it is very hard. Yet I do not want to return to the state I was in before God visited me in this sickness, for I know my inward self has been enriched by this suffering." Doesn't that tell the truth of Jesus' saying? When I am lifted up, I will draw all men unto me. Oh, if only we would allow ourselves to be thus drawn by Jesus. I believe we would then find our happiness.

And now, there is one word I want to emphasize in the saying of our Savior. That is the most mysterious word in the whole sentence: "all." I will draw all men unto me—*all*. We know how few allow themselves to be drawn to him, and we must ask ourselves: Are we among those who allow themselves to be drawn to him? How many insist on going their own way, the way to ruin? And yet our Savior promises: I will draw *all* men to myself. What hope this word gives us! Hope that even those who appear lost will be saved by the power of the cross of Christ, although we cannot understand how. What comfort such a faith is for the heart of many a poor mother who is mourning over a misguided child—and for many others as well. A veil of mystery lies over many questions—but in hope and in faith we grasp the mystery.

{ 3 }

*The Courage of Action**

*And the seventy returned again with joy, saying, Lord,
even the devils are subject unto us through thy name.
And as he said unto them, I beheld Satan as lightning
fall from heaven. Behold, I give unto you power to
tread on serpents and scorpions, and over all the power
of the enemy: and nothing shall by any means hurt you.
Notwithstanding in this rejoice not, that the spirits are
subject unto you; but rather rejoice, because your
names are written in heaven.* LUKE *10:17–21*

IT WAS HARVEST time. Many men had gathered around
Jesus and followed him from village to village. Now they
were getting ready to go back home and gather the harvest.
But from among them he chose seventy whom he knew
well because they had often sat around him (this was after
he had sent out the Twelve). He said to the seventy men:
Go out first and preach the gospel, then come back and I
will let you go.

Seventy, chosen symbolically for the number of the

* *Preached Sunday, May 11, 1902, at the morning service at St.
Nicolai's Church.*

Gentile nations, as they were counted in the Old Testament. None could have been less prepared than they—and yet he commanded them to go and preach. Jesus knew what they would gain by this activity, that something would be revealed to them by preaching the gospel. Nor was he deceived. "We have fought and won!" they cry out jubilantly on their return.

They had fought and won—and now they owned the secret of Christianity. They carried it within them, and no one could take it from them. For Christianity is conflict and victory through Jesus. That is why Jesus praised God in this hour for revealing to the simple the secret which was hidden from the wise and clever.

The revelation was not granted them because of their mere simplicity. They were chosen because they had acted and fought as ordinary people. Not by meditation and reflection does one grasp the great secret which hovers over the world and human life. The higher realization flowers only in work and action. For this highest realization there is no difference between the wise and the simple. The simple, if they act, are given insights kept from the wise.

In action lies wisdom and confidence. A man who does not act gets no further than the maxim: Life means conflict and tribulation. But a man who acts can attain the higher wisdom and know that life is conflict and victory. That is why God forces men to labor. That is why he gives them children to bring up. That is why he gives them duties. Through action, they may reach a deeper realization. They may have confidence and belief in the victory of Christ. You know the beautiful saying: "I lay in heavy chains until you came and set me free."

But how does Jesus approach those who are weighed down by sorrow or remorse? He lays before them a duty, a task. And in executing it they regain, not without hard fight, their confidence and faith. For in action they feel the power of God which preserves and revitalizes everything.

This realization of life is like a man who sits by his window, watching the March wind chase the dark clouds across the sky. "How sad, how desolate," he says, and he gets no further. Meanwhile, a man is working in the field. He sees the wind chasing the clouds, but he grasps more than that. He feels a living breath. He senses life stirring everywhere, the birth of a victorious power which cannot be held back. He alone has understood the March wind, for he was there as a worker in the fertile field. Only those who stand as workers in the field of life notice the life-giving breath and the victorious Spirit of God which rules the world. A man who is active cannot despair of victory of the divine over evil. You have heard of the philosopher Schopenhauer, who in his writings elevated to a supreme wisdom his belief that life is only suffering, conflict, and misery. I can never read a page of his without asking myself what would have become of this man if—instead of being able to withdraw in splendid isolation from any profession—he had been obliged to become a schoolteacher in a small Alpine village where he would have been faced with the task of converting neglected children into useful citizens. He would never have written his famous books. People would never have lionized him or pressed laurel wreaths upon his silver locks. But Schopenhauer's brilliance made him only a wise man. The simple and ignorant men of Galilee whom Jesus had sent out to work possessed a wisdom higher than his. For to them had become manifest the secret that life is conflict and victory in Christ.

They bore this secret also in a more tangible form. They boasted with joy that they had realized it through Jesus' power and strength working in them. They had been able to do signs, to heal the sick, and to cast out demons. Jesus rejoiced with them. Yes, certainly, he tells them, the time of conflict with the power of evil has begun, and we shall be victorious. To help them understand, he speaks in the language of the time. I saw Satan fall as lightning from heaven, he says. Snakes and scorpions cannot poison you, for I have given you power. Nothing will harm you. Then, before giving them a final blessing and sending them back to their homes, he cast a veil over their all-too-confident joy by saying: "Don't rejoice because the spirits are subject unto you. Rather, rejoice because your names are written in heaven." What he meant by this higher, interior joy they did not comprehend.

But they were to understand it later. They returned home, and everyday life with all its trivialities and anxieties engrossed them once more. And there they found themselves in conflict with the power of evil, an evil much greater than the perils they had survived on their mission. It was not a battle against Satan, who dwells in the air and speaks words of blasphemy through the mouth of the possessed. No, it was a struggle against the power of evil which dwelt in their hearts. It was the war against sin, the endeavor to fulfill the saying: "Ye shall be perfect, as your Father in heaven is perfect." It was a fight for purity of heart, for trust in God, for hope in tribulation, for faith. And this silent battle within was difficult, for the eye of Jesus was no longer on them. He was far from them, no longer in this world. But now, in this inner struggle, they at last understood the meaning of his words when they had returned. He had spoken of interior joy. Those words, the last they heard him speak—I have given you power, nothing will harm you, rejoice that your names are written in heaven—they now comprehended as eternal, interior, undying words. They understood them as we understand them, words of the Lord to those in conflict. And still today, in the hearts of those who fight, they shine as brightly as the stars in the sky. "I have given you power"—Christ is a power within the combatants. Who can explain this? Who can explain how his strength and power worked in those days in the missionaries he sent out in Galilee, enabling them to perform work like his? And yet, they experienced it in themselves. So, to this day, Christ is a power in all who from their hearts accept him as their Savior. The power they have within is invisible from the outside, a mysterious power, a power to lead them forward and sustain them.

And this power becomes most evident in us when we accept inward or outward harm. Nothing shall hurt you. The Lord has said so. Nothing, not sorrow or tribulation, not sickness or pain or disappointment. From all these bitter conflicts you will arise strengthened and renewed, enriched in the inner man.

Nothing will harm you—neither the Fall nor sin, Jesus promises. For whoever accepts me as his Savior proceeds, through humiliation and remorse, to joy and forgiveness and a life begun anew.

Hence this eternal promise: Rejoice, for your names are written in heaven—not as those who rest, or as those who suffer, but as those who fight with the promise of victory through Jesus Christ. Rejoice, for you cannot be lost. God holds his protecting hand over you.

As those Galileans went their homeward way, they dreamed of peace and the joy of peace. But in the "Rejoice" he called after them, which they did not understand, there was an echo: I came not to bring peace but a sword. It was a prophetic saying. Later, in trial and tribulation, when the waves closed over their heads, they heard again this powerful word "Rejoice," spoken to those in the midst of conflict and strife. Now they understood it. Rejoice because your names are written in heaven! There was one who was not with them—the apostle Paul—and he did not hear this word "Rejoice." But he proclaimed with the tongue of an angel all the glory that lies within this word. His interpretation of the call to rejoice in the midst of conflict is written in the eighth chapter of the Letter to the Romans:

> What shall we then say to these things? If God be for us, who can be against us? He that spared not his own Son, but delivered him up for us all, how shall he not with him also freely give us all things? Who shall lay any thing to the charge of God's elect? It is God that justifieth. Who is he that condemneth? It is Christ that died, yea rather, that is risen again, who is even at the right hand of God, who also maketh intercession for us. Who shall separate us from the love of Christ? shall tribulation, or distress, or persecution, or famine, or nakedness, or peril, or sword? As it is written, For thy sake we are killed all the day long; we are accounted as sheep for the slaughter. Nay, in all these things we are more than conquerors through him that loved us. For I am persuaded, that neither death, nor life, nor angels, nor principalities, nor powers, nor things present, nor things to come, nor height, nor depth, nor any other creature, shall be able to separate us from the love of God, which is in Christ Jesus our Lord.

{ 4 }

Christic in Our Life[*]

Teaching them to observe all things whatsoever I have commanded you: and, lo, I am with you alway, even unto the end of the world. Amen. MATTHEW 28:20

THIS PROMISE is like the sunrise. It is as though we were standing on a high mountain and saw the farthest peaks and valleys lighted by a ray of the morning sun. I am with you unto the close of the age. This was the last word the Risen One spoke to his disciples. For some of us it might lose part of its beauty because we find it hard to believe that Jesus spoke in human terms to his disciples after his life on earth had come to an end. But, I believe, what really matters is the eternal truth enshrined in these words. The outward form in which the Risen Lord addressed his disciples in order to strengthen and comfort them may be a symbol, a parable. What is crucial to us is that we know what it means, whether we have experienced his promise in our lives: I am with you.

What tremendous inner power exists in spiritual com-

* Preached Sunday, April 24, 1904, at the morning service at St. Nicolai's Church.

munion with another man! How pitiable and destitute men are when they are spiritually alone, when they have no one to understand and encourage them. Doubly pitiable if they don't even feel the need for it!

The older we grow the more we realize that true power and happiness come to us only from those who spiritually mean something to us. Whether they are near or far, still alive or dead, we need them if we are to find our way through life. The good we bear within us can be turned into life and action only when they are near to us in spirit. When I hear the phrase "eternal life," I don't immediately think of the peace and joy of those who have passed from this life. I first think of the eternal life which has become manifest to me as a spiritual presence of those who are no more and of those who are still alive: men whose proximity I feel primarily as spiritual beings rather than earthly existences. When human beings with all their weaknesses and defects can mean so much to us, how much greater is our feeling for him who embraces all that is pure, spiritual, and eternal. In this saying, "I am with you," lies the fate of every human life. Those who can say, "Yes, it is so. I know what his spiritual nearness is"—they are rich and happy beyond expression. Those for whom this promise means nothing relevant and connotes no real experience—they are poor, poor men whether they realize it or not.

But how can we find him? He is there, in the Gospels, in the teachings of the church, truly present. In the Gospels his life on earth is described. In the church's teaching we discover what he means to us. Yet so many pass him by and cannot find him, spending their lives unaware of the reality of his spiritual presence. I speak not only of those who want to believe with all their hearts but cannot yet experience him personally or feel his eye upon them, cannot incorporate their will in his. I also think of those who have not been aware of his presence. Everything they hear or read about spiritual communion with him is meaningless in terms of God's nearness as they sense it, a weak definition of the intensity they feel. For spiritual communion surpasses all description, something to be experienced but never put into adequate words.

And now, how does it come to pass that this Jesus of the Gospels, this Savior of the church's teachings, enters our lives as a living, spiritual being? You will remember how St. Paul says in his letters: "I will speak to you in a human way." So *I* would speak to you in a human way. For I am afraid we don't speak of Jesus in a human way today. Last Good Friday, while we were meditating in deep devotion upon his death, in France someone was removing his picture from the law courts, where until then he had looked down at the judges. Those who gave the order for this could never have heard anyone speak of Jesus in a human way. They heard him referred to in dead formulas and dogmas, so they thought he belonged only to the church, and they did not appreciate his simple human greatness. Often it appears that the world cannot penetrate to Jesus because he is so boxed in by dogmas. It is like a glorious ancient cathedral whose splendor has been made invisible by the houses encroaching upon it. Space must be cleared around Jesus so he becomes accessible.

I may be wrong, but I have the impression that many are waiting in vain to feel his presence, waiting for this promise—I am with you—to become valid in their lives. They wait and wait until finally this living communion, in which true religion really begins, becomes elusive, a goal out of reach, an end they can never realize. In the end they forgo it. If we could see the religious life of those we meet, of many who are with us in church Sunday after Sunday, we would be aware of countless silent unfulfilled yearn-

ings. We would see much resignation in people who have given up hoping they can ever find spiritual communion with Christ, ever know his presence.

Perhaps they have cherished a false picture of him. They expect a Savior to comfort them, and certainly he has manifested himself as the comforter to many who lay in bonds of sin and misfortune. And yet—please don't misunderstand me—to put it inadequately and briefly, isn't it unnatural, I sometimes wonder, for every man to wait for some violent event or inner experience in his life— for example, like that of Augustine or Luther—in order for Jesus to comfort him? This is not the way for everyone. I am convinced that many in our time are waiting for a special need to be comforted, hoping that he will appear to them then; and because they never have the need, he never comes to them and they never find him. How did he come near to the first disciples? Not as a comforting Savior. He does not approach only miserably unhappy men and say to them: "Come, I will comfort you." Rather, he says to men who are healthy and fresh in the midst of life: "Come, I will make you fishers of men. That means you will help me in my life's work." Is it not significant that just before the words of our text: "I am with you alway, even unto the end of the world," we find the command to continue his work: "Go ye into all the world and teach the nations"? The "I" in the "I am with you" is preeminently a demand. It means: I will not let you go; you must continue my life's work. And his promise, "I am with you," continues throughout the world from generation to generation. Only by continuing his life's work, in battle and labor for him, do we realize what is meant by "I am with you." This has not changed. The natural way to him is to take part in his work. By sharing his labors, we enter into ever greater and stronger spiritual communion of personal intercourse with him. Is it not marvelous, this personal communion among men? Those who come close to us become dear to us because the same goal and the same ideal keep us together. We are united with men with whom we have nothing else in common, men we would otherwise fail to understand. This is why our human will must become one with the all-powerful will of Jesus. Then a communion with him will be created, and men will experience the meaning of his promise: "I am with you."

Therefore, if I may proclaim the Christ message in a human way, I would say to all doubters and to all those who yearn in vain to feel his living presence: All right, let everthing else go, as long as you hold fast to this one truth: he is a man who has the right to demand your help in the work he began. If you will do this, his glorious presence will come over you and you will become rich, richer, far richer than you can imagine!

I always return to this thought, and I always begin with it. Like a clearing in the wood, a focal point where all paths meet, it was a comfort and it still is. Those who study theology, some say, must face hard battles because of the doubts that arise when they engage in close study and research into Christian doctrine and its history. I cannot speak of this from experience, for I myself have never for a moment known such a state of mind. I always told myself: Should everything else fail, one thing will remain. We poor weak men may continue his work, and our life, our thought, our aims, and all our actions will thus be hallowed. Isn't that enough—more than enough—for true joy, true blessedness and peace? And because I have been so certain of his spiritual presence, doubts and temptations have never assailed me.

Now you will say: Such religion is lacking in humility. You are treating the Savior as an equal; you are not a broken and contrite man. I believe that contrition and humility come imperceptibly. Who could step into the shadow of a great mountain without feeling insignificant? "I am with you all the days"—there is more in this than meets the eye. It says: I am with you all the days to teach you humility. For what can we possibly do for him that will give us the right to feel we are really serving him? You remember the legend of St. Christopher. When he carried a small child across the river, his burden became heavier and heavier until it weighed him down. St. Christopher said he could bear no greater load and the child replied, "Thou has borne on thy shoulders all the world and him who created it." In Jesus' promise, "I am with you," there is a heavy weight like that. For whoever feels his presence will be weighed down by him. Only those who feel his presence know how unholy and sinful their wills are. Yes, I would say only they truly know what sin is.

And now one last point. Jesus says: I am with you to comfort you and lift you up above the world and all the experiences it brings. Whoever enjoys spiritual communion with him, whoever asks him questions and receives an answer, knows that nothing on earth—no misfortune, no trouble, no suffering—could ever be greater than the comfort he returns. That is how he strengthened his disciples of old in their persecution and loneliness. In the time of battle and in the hour of death, they could hear him say: "I am with you." Is not this assurance, "He is with me," written on every page of the letters of St. Paul? You remember the saying: "I can do all things through him who strengthens me, Christ." Infinite comfort floods over everyone who lives in communion with him. Blessed is he who has found it.

God's goodness toward us is a gift so great that we cannot accept it lightly.

{ 5 }

*Gratitude—the Secret of Life**

*Thou art worthy, O Lord, to receive glory and honour
and power: for thou hast created all things, and for thy
pleasure they are and were created.*

REVELATION 4:11

LAST SUNDAY in the church school I spoke to the children
about the festivals of harvest, autumn, and Thanksgiving.
I asked if any of them had ever harvested anything. One
said he had helped pick apples. Another had helped pick
grapes in a vineyard he did not own. But most of them
had not really experienced the harvest of autumn. They
only knew that it had been a good year. To help them to
understand why we ought to celebrate such a festival, I
reminded them of the saying: "Rejoice with them that do
rejoice."

Even now I almost wish I were standing in a village
church and preaching to people who can calculate before
entering the House of God how much they have harvested,
who perhaps will be going out to their vineyards this very

* Preached Sunday, November 20, 1904, at the morning service at
St. Nicolai's Church.

afternoon to check the plants for next year. Speaking to
them of the joys of harvest would be much easier than
speaking to you city dwellers. For you don't receive anything directly from God's hand. Very few of you have
your own plot of land or even a single tree. It is harder for
us today to feel near to God among the streets and houses
of the city than it is for countryfolk. For them the harvested fields bathed in the autumn mists speak of God
and his goodness far more vividly than any human lips.

Yet I ask you not only to rejoice with those who rejoice,
but also to rejoice on behalf of those who do not themselves rejoice. Many have harvested and gathered into their
barns, yet all reapers are not grateful this day. Within the
limits of this city stand fields which are barren before men.
They are also barren before God, for he has harvested
no thanks from them. That is why we must give thanks
for those who do not thank him themselves. Then the
voice of praise will rise from this valley and be heard
on high.

Why does God need our thanks? This will strike you as
an almost blasphemous question, coming as it does from
the pulpit. But which of you has not asked it himself,
even as a child? I want to ask it in a religious sense. Have
you ever considered what our thanks might mean to God?
I believe we do not give enough thanks because we do not
realize what a great thing it is to give thanks.

It appears that men have always instinctively known that
God needed their thanks. Even on the lowest level of understanding, men have felt the urge to offer him something,
the fruit of their field, of their flocks and herds. Admittedly, they knew that these things belonged to him already,
that it was he who made them and preserved them. Yet
they sensed that because they were offered to him by man,
the sheaves and the beasts meant far more to God than all

the other things which the world produced through his power. With them it was only a vague idea, a rough and ready parable. But for us it is much clearer, much more plain, if indeed we mere mortals can grasp so great a mystery. God needs our thanks. He lives by it. Without our human gratitude he, the eternal, infinite, almighty One, is poor, for his wealth does not return to him.

An earthly ruler, however large his kingdom and however many his subjects, is poor unless he wins the gratitude of those he rules. If he is their sovereign in name only, he is poverty-stricken. So, too, God is poor, although he rules over everything, if the whole wealth of his being, which he put into his creation, does not return to him in the shape of human gratitude. That is why he created something outside of himself, why he is not wrapped up in contemplation of his own solitary being. Why did he create anything apart from himself at all? So that he might experience his own abundance in the life he has created. He, the Almighty, whose will is deed, created beings with wills of their own. Now he waits to see whether they wish to do his will, that his will may be done on earth. The design of the world is completed in their willingness. He waits, too, for the goodness and love he poured into creation to ascend to him again. It may be gratitude when the birds sing and the trees are in bud and a joyful noise sounds over the earth. It may be gratitude when the ripe ears of corn swish against each other and the vines swing heavy with purple fruit under the blue September sky. But this gratitude of the world does not rise above the sphere of the creaturely and ascend to him. God is spirit, and the physical must become spiritualized before it can reach him. All the power, life, and goodness which he put into the world returns to him in proportion to the spiritual thanks offered by men. So, too, the will he placed in creation returns only insofar as it is fulfilled by men. The life and abundance of God consist in the return of his spirit from the world in the spirit of human beings. And whatever does not so return in the spirit of men is lost, imprisoned in creatureliness.

Therefore mark well: the gratitude ascending from man to God is the supreme transaction between earth and heaven. Most men, however, live their daily lives oblivious of this supreme event. They having no inkling that their lives are lost to God because they have not given him thanks. It is just like the parable. Those seeds that fell by the wayside, among stones, and among thorns bore no fruit. But the small amount of seed falling on good ground multiplied thirty, sixty, and a hundredfold, compensating for all that was lost. So it is when we give thanks to God. The goodness he has poured forth upon mankind this year is lost on many, and very few are like the tree planted by the water, which brings forth fruit to God in due season. Even if only those few thousands who are gathered in the churches of our land thank him truly from the bottom of their hearts, this is a rare and rich fruit to him.

But to give thanks is not only a happening that embraces the whole purpose of creation within itself; it is also an experience. He who thanks God with his whole heart experiences something. He is himself enriched. All too often we think we are destitute of joy and fortune. Our lives seem empty and unsatisfied, and we know not why. Now take a look at yourselves. The times of poverty within are the times when you do not give thanks to God. What life brings has no value in itself. It acquires value only by our giving thanks to God. Today at the harvest Thanksgiving it is not those who have gathered much into their barns who are rich. Those who thank God much are the truly wealthy. So our inner happiness depends not on what we experience but on the degree of our gratitude to God, whatever the experience. Your life is something opaque, not transparent, as long as you look at it in an ordinary human way. But if you hold it up against the light of God's goodness, it shines and turns transparent, radiant and bright. And then you ask yourself in amazement: Is this really my own life I see before me?

He who does not reflect his life back to God in gratitude does not know himself. The true wealth of our lives is hidden from our natural senses. The ears of corn can be seen only when they are spread out before God.

And not only riches but also power shall be yours through communion with God. Even among men, gratitude creates an intimate communion. Gratitude is ultimately such a strong bond that nothing can break it. How much more so with God. Because we fail to give thanks, we do not have communion with him. That is why he seems so far away. The sacrifice which reconciles us with him and binds us to him is lacking. We know the saying: "Call upon me in the time of trouble; so will I hear thee and thou shalt praise me." We have no doubt experienced it, but we forget the other part: "Offer unto God thanksgiving." To pray means first to give thanks, and many never achieve true communion with him in their prayers because they do not begin with thanksgiving. As you know, our Lord Jesus was always with God, knew him to be near, and understood him in all his ways because he was constantly giving thanks. His loving gratitude raised him to the Father. And you, too, can partake of this happiness when you start thanking God from the depths of your hearts. When your gratitude ascends to God, you yourselves are lifted up above a worldly view of life, and everything below you disappears from sight. You realize how your life rests in him. You see the world as it is in him.

What before seemed hard becomes easy. What was an unsurmountable hurdle in your way is flattened out, and you return to your daily life as a different man. Happy are they who in gratitude to God are armed for life.

So, when you feel weak, downcast, and sad, start giving thanks. Things will then go better. Force yourself to do it. And if your heart angrily objects and asks: What's the good? don't let it rest. Make it search then and there for something, anything, to be grateful for. Once you have found the first thing, other things will follow, and finally you will find yourself giving endless thanks.

The greatest thing is to give thanks for everything. He who has learned this knows what it means to live. He has penetrated the whole mystery of life: giving thanks for everything. If you do not own fields or meadows, take the giving of thanks at this harvest festival as a parable. That's what our Lord did, and he too did not own fields. He took everything in nature as a parable and so owned it in spirit. We offer up thanksgiving this day for the fruits of the earth. We thank God for the sunshine, but also for the hard rain that satisfies the thirst of earth, for the driving wind that carries the pollen from one plant to another, for the cold that preserved the seed in the earth, for the storms of spring that washed the land of snow and ice. Thus you give thanks to God not only for the happy and sunny events which ripen your life's fruit. Much that is sad and hard is also mixed in with life's blessings. And for that you must thank God, because it, too, has contributed to your spiritual growth. If life is such a burden that you feel crushed beneath it, then search out how you can thank God nonetheless. For sometimes we are blind to God's plan for us and receive our sight only when we try to thank him.

You who are fortunate, help those who must struggle

and prevail until they reach their goal through the prayer of gratitude you offer up. Sometimes, when I stand before the altar and say the opening prayer, I feel there must be some among you who have had a glorious experience during the past week. Then it seems to me that your thoughts, rising around the words of my prayers, form wonderful harmonies around a simple melody. By your thoughts the prayers of the downcast are strengthened and lifted up through space in gratitude to God.

{ 6 }

Compelling Hope*

*And Jesus said unto him, No man, having put his hand
to the plough, and looking back, is fit for the kingdom
of God.*   LUKE 9:62

YOU ALL KNOW what precedes this text. Some people determined to follow Jesus, and he forbade them to do what
seemed natural to them. One wanted to put his house in
order first and say goodbye, but Jesus would not allow
him to do so. The other wanted to bury his father first,
but the Lord said to him: "Let the dead bury their dead."

What Jesus demands is not just. But that is how it is
with the kingdom of God. For the sake of the kingdom,
matters which seem pressing to our natural human judgment are untimely in light of more important events.

Every Advent I wonder why the people of Israel—who,
more than any other race, yearned with passion for the
coming of the Redeemer, who celebrated a glorious Advent, who prepared so well for the kingdom of God—
lost it when it came. It was not from a dearth of piety, not

---

* Preached Sunday, December 18, 1904, at the morning service at St.
Nicolai's Church.

from hardheartedness; rather, it was because of their untimely devotion to the law and the prophets. They did not understand the signs of the times, and so the Lord Jesus himself could not help them.

Once again a great time of Advent came at the end of the Middle Ages, when men's spirits were waiting in suspense. Time, like a chomping horse, stood harnessed to the plow, breathing fire, and the morning clouds reddened the skies. But they looked back to the Church Fathers and councils and remained where they were.

And so we have in our midst Judaism and Catholicism; both looked back and were prevented from following the Lord by perfectly natural and human loyalties. Admittedly there is much excellent and efficient piety in these religions, many noble aspirations and genuine resources. But they are not compatible with the kingdom of God. They remain fettered by out-of-date ideas. They are not the salt of the earth. And when the salt has lost its savor, wherewith shall it be salted?

For I am always afraid that as we stand in the midst of an Advent season we might miss its significance because we look back. Maybe it is not Advent after all? I hear of blasphemy and judgment. Now we read in Scripture that when blasphemy and judgment increase, the time is fulfilled and he will reappear in the world. Amid the blasphemy and the accusations against the medieval church, the Christ of the Reformation appeared. So listen. Perhaps above the derisive noise of scorn about Christianity in the world today you may hear the Lord coming. Perhaps this will be the third great Advent! Don't look back! Look ahead! There may be a shining figure standing before the plow.

But I am afraid we do look back. We spend far too much time discussing the Reformers. We believe it will strengthen our age if we revive the age of the Reformation in every possible way, with all its heroic figures—as though that would renew and strengthen us in our work. We spend too much time celebrating the past. As we hear our times speak, we are inclined to say: Less Luther, less Gustavus-Adolphus, more Christ.

I would never boldly declare that there is too much worship of the Reformers had not Christ's word forbade us to look back—and if he had not used such harsh language to the man who wanted to bury his father first: "Let the dead bury their dead. Don't let piety deceive you about the real duty of this moment." A monk recently wrote a scathing and quite unfair book about Luther,* and now nearly every week we witness the release of some new publication in the defense of Luther, as though that were the task of Protestantism. Why? Does he need it? Let the dead bury their dead! And don't bring back the times when angels fought the devil for a corpse. He may keep the corpse, for the spirit is alive. The time is ripe for greater things than pious exercises.

Are we really deceiving ourselves? Our times put such great stress on certain things, believing that because they are prompted by our natural instincts they are timely for the kingdom of God. Just look: it is only the cry of "Let us first" which our Lord cuts short with an impatient word. It is as though we had said: Let us first come to grips with Catholicism and then, when Protestantism has gained strength against its adversaries, we will go ahead. Or: Let us first vindicate Christianity against the attacks of science. Or: Let us first discover modern formulas. Let us replace the old creed with the modern

* Albert Schweitzer is alluding here to H. Denifle's book *Luther und Luthertum in der ersten Entwicklung*, which appeared in 1904, evoking great controversy as well as numerous replies.—U.N.

spirit in order to reconcile ourselves with the gospel. Then we will tackle the new tasks. Or: Let us first create new organizations. Let us reconcile the Protestant churches and achieve reunion. Then a new time will dawn for the gospel.

But see: Preoccupied with these timely tasks we forget the untimely ones; preoccupied with this age, we forget the future—but the kingdom of God is untimely labor for the future.

Which of us can judge this noble, gallant age of ours without first condemning himself? We all labor with this timely warning: "Let us first." What we are short of is men who are great enough to judge the noble endeavors of our age, men who have the right to be unjust to us. The great men of the Advent are missing. But the world judges and jeers. However unfair the situation, in the end we have to hold our peace and face humiliation. For the world is right about one thing: Christianity is powerless in our time, and because it has no power it is judged. Admittedly, the word of God is preached and the Scriptures are taught. But the gospel is like glorious seed blown about in the air, dropping to the ground everywhere but sprouting nowhere because there are no men to plow the furrow. So the birds of the heavens come and eat it up and it is lost to the world.

We must become good plowmen. Hope is the prerequisite of plowing. What sort of farmer plows the furrow in the autumn but has no hope for the spring? So, too, we accomplish nothing without hope, without a sure inner hope that a new age is about to dawn. Hope is strength. The energy in the world is equal to the hope in it. And even if only a few people share such hopes, a power is created which nothing can hold down—it inevitably spreads to others.

The second essential of plowing is silence. We must learn that all of our talking and planning is powerless. Modest, quiet work in the kingdom of God is the order of the day.

The third need when plowing is to work in solitude. We expect all kinds of salvation from meetings, congresses, and organized cooperation. But we deceive ourselves. The most blessed labors can only be accomplished alone, and that is just what we must learn—to work independently. Even if several plowmen plow one field, each follows his own plow. They do not talk to one another; each sees his neighbor and senses the nearness of his fellow worker, all bound together in a common, wordless task.

To hope, to keep silent, and to work alone—that is what we must learn to do if we really want to labor in the true spirit. But what exactly does it involve, this plowing? The plowman does not pull the plow. He does not push it. He only directs it. That is just how events move in our lives. We can do nothing but guide them straight in the direction which leads to our Lord Jesus Christ, striving toward him in all we do and experience. Strive toward him, and the furrow will plow itself.

That is what men sense in us if the power of Christianity emanates from us. We must look for him in everything that comes our way and in everything we do. Instead of letting our lives be tossed to and fro by the natural course of things, we must pursue a straight line.

When I was a boy I wanted to learn to plow. I thought it would be easy—all I would have to do to direct the plow was to grasp the handles. I found that to make a furrow I had to put my whole weight to the plow. Often in the course of my life I have discovered that nothing else will suffice, and no furrow will be turned unless we do it with all our might. We must take life seriously. I regard that as an obligation we owe to Jesus. I want others to sense that we take life seriously. I want them to see that every moment we are conscious of our responsibility to our Lord for what our existence means to the people around us and what it means for the coming of the kingdom of God in the world. There is nothing depressing about this responsibility. No, there is something joyous in it, something that makes us strong. People must notice how we wrestle and strive to serve our Lord worthily in the world. If we are strong, they will sense the breath of a higher world within us. And if we are weak, they will not blaspheme the name of God because of our shortcomings. For they will know we are striving to do our best. Because it sets its goals so high, Christianity has a right to expect indulgence in the world. But it gets it only when people see that Christians are fighting a serious battle.

There is something very strange about "taking life seriously." He who leans heavily on the plow sees a wave of green sprouting forth and leafing out from under the plowshare. With simple pressure he buries weeds which he could not otherwise have uprooted. A dozen workers could not have cleared the field in one day, but the plowman can do it in a few hours! In much the same way all the temptations you find along the way get buried if you take life seriously. People who live like that have an easier life than other men, just because they take it seriously in order to plow a furrow for Jesus. And their passage brings cleansing and purification and helps others to fight. The battle is hard only for those who have none of the goals that make life difficult.

When a man has accomplished something, it is said in the language of the world: He has made his mark. People know what he has done. Our Lord Jesus sets before us a different goal, to plow a furrow. That means to do something full of blessing, an act whose initial significance will vanish. When the ears of corn wave in the field, who notices the furrow anymore? Who surveys this golden sea and remembers the names of those who plowed the furrows? But all the same, the plowmen did their job under the dark autumn skies. While the storm howled and the clouds scurried along, they plowed their furrow in hope.

Like them, we should be quiet and modest and plow our furrow, looking toward the Lord and taking our lives seriously. Will this make the earth ready for the new sowing? And when we are no longer present, will our furrow be concealed by the life that springs up out of it?

{ 7 }

*The Call to Mission**

And Jesus said unto them, Come ye after me, and I will make you to become fishers of men.   MARK *1:17*

On THIS DAY in the ancient church the Feast of the Epiphany was celebrated. It was the feast of the manifestation of Christ, the most ancient and most revered of festivals. Only later was it overshadowed by the Feast of Christmas, until finally it lost all its splendor. Celebrants of the Feast of Epiphany rejoiced in the revelation of Christ's glory on earth, his revelation as Savior.

In our country we keep our missionary festival this day, and rightly so. Of course it is not actually a festival, for festivals are celebrated in memory of some great event of the past. Here nothing done in the past is significant, for almost everything remains to be done. And nowadays there is very little to suggest a special celebration in our churches. Epiphany is no different from any ordinary Sunday.

* *Preached Sunday, January 6, 1905, at the morning service at St. Nicolai's Church.*

Yet it is a festival. But it is very different from those noisy memorial days of which there are more than enough in our time, festivals in which the past is elevated to heaven and afterward everyone comes down to earth with a bump, when everything is turned back to front. Today is, rather, a commemoration: we look forward, not remembering the past but looking to the present and the future, prepared to lend a hand in shaping what must come to be.

You have no more illusions than I about the popularity of missionary work. Even otherwise good and rightminded people shun any association with missions. I recently heard a gentleman in Paris who is much given to good works tell a lady who was collecting for a good cause, "Come at any time. You will always find an open door and an open hand. Only don't ever ask anything for missions. I never give a cent—it's money thrown down the drain."

Perhaps some of you don't regard missions very highly. You have never faced up to the subject properly.

Consider my own experience over the past few years. How often I have got into an argument about missions— over land and sea, traveling by road and by train, on mountaintops and in the plains, with friends and with strangers. I make it a matter of principle never to allow a thoughtless remark about missions to pass unnoticed in my presence. Thus I have a pretty good idea why people are so opposed to missions.

I want to tell you my reason for standing up for missions —just a few words to counteract some people's prejudices maybe, but especially that you may know how to reply if somebody should ever say anything against missions in your presence. If ever a preacher who Sunday by Sunday lays bare his thoughts and his heart has the right to ask you for something, I now ask you this one thing. Never permit in your presence any thoughtless talk or grumbling about missionary work. Never allow such opinions to go unanswered.

The first objection we always hear is this: Why don't you leave people to their own religion? Uprooting them from the faiths which until now have made them happy only disturbs them. To this I reply: For me, missionary work in itself is not primarily a religious matter. Far from it. It is first and foremost a duty of humanity never realized or acted upon by our states and nations. Only religious people, only simple souls, have undertaken it in the name of Jesus.

What do our people and nations think about when they gaze across the sea? Of countries to be taken under their so-called protection or otherwise annexed? Of what they might siphon out of the country—always to their advantage? But how they can make those human beings really human, how they can teach them to work and acquire civilization, how civilizations can be developed so that contact with other cultures does not destroy them—that is something these states never consider. Our own states, with all the culture they boast, look very different from the other viewpoint. We are robber states. And where are the people in our civilized states who will undertake long-term, selfless labor to educate other peoples and bring them the blessings of our culture? Where are the workmen, tradesmen, teachers, professors, and doctors who will go to these countries and work there to achieve the blessings of culture? What efforts does our society make in that direction? None at all. Only a few poor missionaries with all their limitations have undertaken a work that our whole society should have been eager to do. Missionaries, not the heads of our elegant and boastful culture, deserve the laurel wreath. They have worked humanly for decades to raise the standards of other people, without primarily giving thought to making their religion understood.

Why? Because to be a disciple of Jesus is the only culture, in which a human being is always a human being, always someone who has a right to the assistance and sacrifice of his fellow men. But our culture divides people into two classes: civilized men, a title bestowed on the persons who do the classifying; and others, who have only the human form, who may perish or go to the dogs for all the "civilized men" care.

Oh, this "noble" culture of ours! It speaks so piously of human dignity and human rights and then disregards this dignity and these rights of countless millions and treads them underfoot, only because they live overseas or because their skins are of different color or because they cannot help themselves. This culture does not know how hollow and miserable and full of glib talk it is, how common it looks to those who follow it across the seas and see what it has done there, and this culture has no right to speak of personal dignity and human rights. Until culture wakes up to its own mission and does something about it, let no one say a word against missions. Missionaries were the ones who stepped in and did their best. True religion is also true humanitarianism. So the missions stepped in the breach for our culture, for our civilization, for our society —and they did for other people what all the other agencies should have done.

If someone were to ask me why I consider Christianity to be the highest and only religion, I would discard all we have learned about comparative religions and their relative worth, and how to judge the strong points of each, and I would say only this: The first command the Lord gave upon earth can be condensed to only one word: *man.* He does not speak of religion, of faith, of the soul, or of anything else on earth; he speaks only of man. "I will make you fishers of men." It is as though he were speaking to all centuries to come: First see to it, I beg you, that man does not perish. Go after him as I went after him and find him where he is, where others have not found him, in filth, in neglect, in indignity. Live with him and help him to become man again.

Jesus has welded religion and humanity so closely together that religion no longer exists as a separate entity; without true humanity, there is no religion. And the challenge of true humanity can no longer be heard without religion.

This human appreciation of missions must prevail. You must stand up for it and labor so that it will prevail.

Many of the objections against missionary work will then fall to the ground.

People say there is still so much to be done at home that missionary work should wait until everything has been accomplished here. There are enough heathens to be converted at home.

So I myself will wait until we have supplied the missionary effort with more skilled people than I can actually afford.

A man once said to me," We need money for all the good that needs to be done at home. I won't give a dime for missionary work." Knowing him well, I asked him whether he gave more for good causes at home, since he did not send anything abroad, and how much he contributed every year to these worthy causes. We continued our walk, and he remained silent. So did I. But since then, the missions have been getting money from him.

What should we answer when they say that missionary work doesn't do any good, that it only squanders money and manpower for nothing? Of course one could tell a long story about the successes of missionary work. One could tell of its accomplishments in the Great Lakes District of Central Africa, what it has done in the South Sea Islands, the hundreds and hundreds of busy, untroubled villages it has created, how it has put a stop to bloodshed, and much more than that. But no. For missionary work is carried on without thought of success. It goes on because it must, out of a compelling force that is the very nature of things where the Spirit of Jesus is.

Ordinary men in everyday life calculate the chances of success; they will undertake a project only if they are confident of reward. But when something is done in Jesus' name, the only thing to take into account is the "must," that mysterious "must" that Jesus keeps insisting on when he talks of the destiny of the Son of man, of the death that awaited him. The less our prospect of success, the greater the force of that "must."

So let us not be sparing in our contributions in money or manpower. Nothing will ever be wasted. And even if it should be buried in the sea or in the desert, it will still be hallowed by the death of Jesus. His death removed the sting from those painful words: "in vain." When he died, men could say, "This person threw himself away and lived in vain"—and yet out of his death came strength. All that is done while following in his footsteps, the effort that seems to be done in vain, bears sacred fruit a thousandfold.

Finally, missionary work is simply an atonement for the crimes of violence done in the name of Christian nations. I will not enumerate all the crimes that have been committed under the pretext of justice. People robbed native inhabitants of their land, made slaves of them, let loose the scum of mankind upon them. Think of the atrocities that were perpetrated upon people subserviated to us, how systematically we have ruined them with our alcoholic "gifts," and everything else we have done. What have the German people done in South West Africa to bring about this revolt? What are we doing now? We decimate them, and then, by the stroke of a pen, we take their land so they have nothing left at all.

I will not discuss this, for I always get the reply: "Well, it could not be helped. In this world, force rules."

All right, but if all this oppression and all this sin and shame are perpetrated under the eye of the German God, or the American God, or the British God, and if our states do not feel obliged first to lay aside their claim to be "Christian"—then the name of Jesus is blasphemed and made a mockery. And the Christianity of our states is blasphemed and made a mockery before those poor people. The name of Jesus has become a curse, and our Christianity —yours and mine—has become a falsehood and a disgrace, if the crimes are not atoned for in the very place where they were instigated. For every person who committed an atrocity in Jesus' name, someone must step in to help in Jesus' name; for every person who robbed, someone must bring a replacement; for everyone who cursed, someone must bless.

In two years about 15,000 troops of the Christian German Empire were sent out among the blacks. About 1,500 died. When will we, the Christian Germany, send out there 15,000 fighters for Jesus, the Lord of mankind? Only then will our name of "Christian" be redeemed—a little, anyhow.

Once, in the mid-nineties, Professor Lucius, a devoted friend of missions who died tragically at a young age, was lecturing about the history of missions on a summer afternoon between three and four o'clock. It was very hot, and barely a half dozen students were present. In his words that day I heard, for the first time, the idea of atonement.

It was so strange. Dogmatics and New Testament exegesis found it difficult to explain why Jesus died for the sins of the world. Everything we had been told about the crucifixion was cut and dried, lifeless. And we could tell that those who lectured on the subject were not too confident about its meaning themselves. But now, as a call to service in Jesus' name, the significance of missions became alive. The word cried so loudly that we could not escape understanding and grasping it. And from that day on, I understood Christianity better and knew why we must work in the mission field.

And now, when you speak about missions, let this be your message: We must make atonement for all the terrible crimes we read of in the newspapers. We must make atonement for the still worse ones, which we do *not* read about in the papers, crimes that are shrouded in the silence of the jungle night. Then you preach Christianity and missionary work at the same time. I implore you to preach it.

{ 8 }

The Life of Service*

And straightway Jesus constrained his disciples to get into a ship, and to go before him unto the other side, while he sent the multitudes away. And when he had sent the multitudes away, he went up into a mountain apart to pray; and when the evening was come, he was there alone. But the ship was now in the midst of the sea, tossed with waves: for the wind was contrary. And in the fourth watch of the night Jesus went unto them, walking on the sea. And when the disciples saw him walking on the sea, they were troubled, saying, It is a spirit; and they cried out for fear. But straightway Jesus spake unto them, saying, Be of good cheer; it is I; be not afraid. And Peter answered him and said, Lord, if it be thou, bid me to come unto thee on the water. And he said, Come. And when Peter was come down out of the ship, he walked on the water, to go to Jesus. But when he saw the wind boisterous, he was afraid; and beginning to sink, he cried, saying, Lord, save me. And immediately Jesus stretched forth his hand, and caught

* Preached Sunday, November 19, 1905, at the morning service at St. Nicolai's Church.

him, and said unto him, O thou of little faith, where-
fore didst thou doubt? And when they were come into
the ship, the wind ceased. MATTHEW *14:22–32*

As you know, this story is only a parable. For if you know
our Lord Jesus and his ways, you know how careful he was
to avoid impressing people by outward signs. It would
have seemed trivial to him to reveal his glory in such a way.
There may be some of us who cling to the letter of
Scripture and feel obliged to believe that Jesus literally
walked upon the water, as though on firm sand, and that
Peter did, too. But even such pedantics agree that the
significance of the event is not to be found in the bare fact
of its happening but, rather, in the permanent spiritual
meaning the parable or miracle has for us. Let us consider
this spiritual meaning.

The disciples wonder whether what they see on the
water is the living Jesus or only an apparition. Why? Because they are so far from him that he cannot join them
physically nor they him. They had been separated from
him once before when he sent them out. But then they
knew every moment that their own feet were able to bring
them back to him, and they had no doubt and no anxiety.
Now, however, water and darkness separate them. The
current and the storm drive them back, making approach
impossible. So they are scared. They think the figure that
is emerging quite close to them out of the darkness must
be an apparition.

We are those disciples. Behind us lies a time when we
felt him to be near us and we could reach out for his hand
at any time: the time of childhood innocence. Now we are
driven out into life and have become aware of what lies
between him and us. Centuries divide us. The darkness of

two millennia hides him from us. And still more of a handicap: the current of our age is against him and drives us back.

Don't you have the feeling that mankind in our day is being driven away from him? How noticeable is the decline in church life during the past ten years. Where is the living church in which we might find Jesus alive and working in spirit, where we might say, "Here he is! This is where we want to be"? The trend of the times and the movement of contemporary thought have overcome Christianity and are driving it off course. No longer is spiritual power the ideal —a force that blesses our mores and our customs, shows our age its noble tasks, and helps it to accomplish them. If Christianity still accounts for anything in public life, its fame exists in political claims and in the charges that the denominations bring against each other before the judgment seat of the rulers and public opinion. And yet our age cannot quite get rid of Jesus. The tide may wash men far away from the shore upon which he walks, but again and again he reappears. An apparition, they say. A man of whom his disciples say: He was risen from the dead— now he cannot die but only walk about like a ghost. An apparition! They say it sarcastically, but in their heart of hearts they have a secret fear that he may conquer the world and win them over, bringing to an end the pleasures they indulge in. They say it in hatred because they have been led astray by what the Christian religion has become in our time. All they see in him is one who is powerless to create spiritual life. An apparition, only an apparition. They say it wistfully, for they wish he would come to their aid and bring the benefits our age so sorely needs. He alone would be able to help, and they think to themselves: If only he were alive and could help us! If only he were not merely an ideal figure, powerless to influence the world.

Thus our world drifts away from him and cannot believe that he is alive. Yet he alone could help! And the world drags us away with it. We seek the living Jesus in what he is doing for our age, and we cannot find him. We sometimes feel like a man just awaking from a dream, trying to decide whether what he has just seen really happened or was only an event in his mind while asleep. Is it not a dream, a chimera, a figment of the imagination, a meaningless conditioned response, to believe that Jesus is the living Lord of our own and of every age? How can we be sure that nothing will make us doubt it? We pose this question not only because we see him impotent in the world, but also because our own innermost world, our own lives, are untouched by his power. We all sense that our life is true life only when it is touched by something greater than ourselves. And this greater can only be He. In certain moments we think we must be able to force him to come and help us, moments when it seems as if we are drowning. We see him, but he does not come closer to help us. And we cry out like Peter, "Lord, is it you?"

For one man it is the turbulent thoughts that seethe within his breast—storms that cannot be seen from the outside. He is looking for direction, for something to hold onto, for joy to sustain his life. The possessions which ought to have provided him this have lost their value, and he seeks something to live for. He feels as though he is drifting, as if he has lost contact with his own depth. He feels as if he is about to be washed up like a corpse on a deserted shore—if Jesus does not save him. Another man wrestles with temptation, knowing that he cannot prevail unless Jesus is alive and grasps him by the hand. Another feels he must reconcile himself to the loss of something that life has taken away from him, something he had to sacrifice. He must conquer despair, knowing that he can find no comfort or peace unless Jesus is alive and comes to him.

Thus life brings to everyone an hour when his anxiety and his superficial faith fall away from him. Then he becomes genuinely devout, and the puzzle the tempter put to Jesus comes to his mind: If you are really alive, if you are not just a name or an idea which mankind has carried along with it for centuries, come and help me.

People will say to you: "Jesus won't come!" You know this feeling yourself. He does not come, any more than he came of old to the disciples as they battled with wind and storm. He lets you go on struggling, sinking more deeply into despair.

But here, in the parable, Jesus took a man by the hand and saved him! Note, however, the question this man asked him: "Lord, if it is you, command me to come to you upon the water." Jesus did not reply, "Don't be impertinent." He simply said, "Come here." This "Come here" occurs not only in this parable but also in the saying in which he promises comfort and strength to those who labor and are heavy-laden. "Come to me, all of you who are heavily laden." In answer to the question, "Is it you?" he says, "Come, come straight to me, across the water!"

It is not pleasant to be a parish minister in this troubled and indifferent age of ours. We would like to impart to modern men something of spirituality. We would like to bring Jesus to them. But we cannot do it. Modern man implores us to dissolve his doubts while at the same time he makes no effort to help himself. And if preaching the gospel consisted of dissolving doubts or of defending a doctrine, the preacher's job would be the most depressing and frustrating thing in the world. It would be like trying to make people rich by counting out their riches for them on paper. But preaching is something quite different, something far more wonderful. For our message is an entirely different matter. It says: Don't just stand there! Go and walk toward him! And this gospel can be preached with joy and confidence, because those who earnestly seek him and are ready to meet him are bound to find him. They simply can't help it. No one can help you. But you, you must do it yourselves. Don't look ahead or behind. Don't listen to what they say or teach. Instead, fix your eye on him and go straight toward him. Don't stop. Search out the path to him. Don't wonder whether this path is safe or feasible, a way made smooth for the ordinary human being. Only make sure that it leads straight to Jesus. Peter was able to come to him only by casting aside all human scruples. But we let them hold us back. Only he who knows that Jesus means more to him than anything else that life can offer is able to step forward with confidence. Only for such a man is the way of life the way to the living Jesus. He who walks there with the inner certainty that all that befalls him—joy and sadness, weakness and strength, all hardship—is inevitable, and that only one thing can have power over him, only he is able to grasp the hand of the living Jesus. Before a man can walk over the uncharted depth which separates him from Jesus, he must first have rejected the ordinary way of looking at life. A man weighed down with ordinary thoughts would lose courage and sink. What gave Peter the strength to walk over the billowing waves as though on firm sand? The desire to reach Jesus. And if you have this desire and inwardly demand of life this one thing, just this single thing, to reach Jesus, then you are captain of your life. The laws and limitations of nature can no longer prevail against you.

This is not theory but life. For with every step you feel you are getting nearer to him. A man does nothing for the Lord's sake without being aware that he has done it for the living Lord. Do you really want to believe in Jesus? Then you must do something for him. In this age of doubt there is no other way to him. And if for Jesus' sake you do even the smallest service to a fellowman, being able to love him by calling secretly on the name of the Lord, if you have given your neighbor a morsel of bread or a sip of water or a piece of garment—those smallest acts of kindness which he promised to bless as though they were done to him—you will see then that you have really done it for him. For then he will come nearer to you, as one who is alive.

I can speak of these little deeds of service because Jesus expressly said that he blesses them with his living presence. It is as though he knew men needed encouragement if they were to walk on the path to him. Everything you force yourself to do in his name compels him to come near to you, as if by a magic word.

You become impatient when someone takes up your time for a quarter of an hour, precious minutes you needed for yourself. But you make yourself give it up for Jesus' sake. Then you have a feeling as if someone is standing behind you and looking at you. You know that Jesus is alive because he has taken something away from you. The dead don't take anything. Yes, every time you whisper, "For his sake"—in little and easy things as well as in great and difficult ones—that is the way to him. No one can describe how the way will be for you. No one can say what "for his sake," the watchword with which the Lord bids you come to him, will mean for you. It will be one way for some, another way for others.

Some weeks ago I heard someone say, "Some are born to

be men of action, others to suffer." That was a remark of resignation. It was an illustration of the saying that there are some people from whom Jesus requires action, others from whom he requires suffering for his sake. If only, in order to come to him, they are ready to give him what he asks!

No one who wants to come to Jesus will perish. At the very moment when Peter was sinking and cried out, "Lord, help me!" Jesus took him by the hand. And he was rescued, safe and sound. How the storm abated we are not told. There is no mention of any magic that Jesus might have used. All we hear is that the storm subsided. When a man finds Jesus, all storms abate.

And what kind of a living man is Jesus? Don't search for formulas to describe him, even if they be hallowed by centuries. I almost got angry the other day when a religious man said to me that only the man who believes in the resurrection of the body and in the glorified body of the risen Christ can believe in the living Jesus.

Jesus is alive for all those who let themselves be guided by him in things both great and small, as though he were still walking in our midst. He says to them, "Do this," or, "Do that." And they answer, "Yes," and go quietly and do as they were bidden, as though the Lord were right in front of them and they could see his form with their spiritual eyes and hear his command with their spiritual ears. The fact that the Lord makes demands on us in our own day is proof to me, the only proof, that he is not a ghost or dead. He is alive. For the sake of those who are searching in our time, let me say: Don't handicap yourself with formulas and doctrines. Have the courage to make your way to him.

Let me explain it in my way. The glorified body of Jesus is to be found in his sayings. For he said of these, "Heaven and earth will pass away, but my words will not pass away." And this is the bodily form in which his spirit is constantly incarnated within the human spirit. This is how he offers himself to men in the Holy Communion. This is what he meant when he consecrated the bread and the wine to be his eternal body and blood. That is his Real Presence, where a man in spiritual hunger and thirst has taken the word of Jesus into himself in order to love. This word was intended for him, for that is where the living Jesus bound himself to that word. His life passed into the life of man, creating peace and joy.

{ 9 }

*Overcoming Death**

*For he must reign, till he hath put all enemies under
his feet. The last enemy that shall be destroyed is death.*
I CORINTHIANS *15:25–26*

THE REIGN OF CHRIST will issue victory over death, the last
enemy, says the apostle Paul in this passage.

This is a good time for us to think about the kingdom of
God. How far has it progressed among us? How far has the
last enemy been overcome? A short while ago the graves
in the churchyards were decorated with the late flowers of
autumn, so sad and beautiful, and people made pilgrimages
to the cemeteries. We watched the last leaves fall. In the
evening a few were still left in the topmost branches, but
by morning there were none. All the living things that had
sprouted and bloomed succumbed to death. They were
alive, but they belonged to death. They were only waiting
for their time. Now death gathers its harvest, and nothing
can withstand it. All this reminds us that life and all its
joys, mankind and ourselves included, are subject to death.

** Preached Sunday, November 17, 1907, at the morning service at St.
Nicolai's Church.*

When we share the experience of the decay of nature, we too feel drawn into the same cycle, and we shudder as though the shroud of death were touching our flesh.

At some time you must have stood on a bridge and watched the water rushing past below, on and on. It seemed as though the bridge were moving, didn't it? Everything around you seemed to be on the move. You braced yourself, you grasped the rail, seized by an unaccountable fear, wondering if there was anything firm left to grasp. Once you clung to the rail, you awoke as out of a nightmare. You get the same feeling when you gaze into the stream of decay and death around you. Here, however, there is nothing firm to grasp, nothing to brace yourself against, no way to escape the feeling of being carried away.

When we were boys we used to play in the dry riverbed during the summer. We jumped from boulder to boulder until we reached the arch of the bridge. There we tested the echo of our voices and stretched up and reached that black line, the high-water mark.

There were white boulders all around, making large islands. I would reach them by wading through the shallow waters lapping around them. When I got to one of them I would listen to the quiet gurgling of the stream. Then I would get frightened. What if the waters should swell and the floods come now? My way to the river's edge would be cut off. Why shouldn't the floods come right now? Why not? Who knows? The big boys would laugh at me and say, "It's midsummer, and there is no more snow on the mountains." I would look away toward the far mountain range. There the peaks lay, bathed by the sun in a blue mist, so peaceful. I fought off my fear but could not get rid of it altogether.

We all walk along the dry riverbed, but no one can say, "It is summer and there won't be any floods." We see one island flooded, then another, all around us. Men are suddenly carried off by hundreds, by thousands. We watch the water rising slowly and relentlessly around one or another close to us, until in an agony of fear he is swept away. That is why the main question in life is: How do you feel about death? Everything that captivates us and engages us is only of relative and temporary worth. In an instant, in the very next hour, it may become utterly valueless.

Death reigns outside. It reigns over you. Does death reign inside you, or have you conquered it within and settled your account with it?

In days gone by, it was considered Christian to heighten men's fear and dread of death. A famous chaplain in a French king's court once pointed from the pulpit to the vaults where the nobility were buried, lying in a row one next to the other along the wall of the royal chapel where the service was being held. He described to them how the dead used to sit there in times past in all their finery, as full of life and gaiety as were his listeners. He told them that they, too, would some day be under those stones, decaying and rotting away. And after painting that gruesome picture, he thought his congregation was now ready for a sermon on repentance and eternal life. But what had he preached to them? The sovereignty of death! Where there is terror and fear of death, there death reigns. I never felt that so strongly as when I visited the Trappist monastery at Oelenberg, where every picture and every stone speaks of death.

This clinging in fear and terror to the hope of eternal life is *not* the victory over death the apostle is talking about. When he tells us that the kingdom of Christ will destroy the power of death, this is only part of what he is saying.

For centuries sermons have been preached on the terror of death in order to frighten men into believing in eternal life. And the result? Numbness, numbness. What a strange and fateful phenomenon! In all spheres of life, anything repeated over and over again loses its effect. A ball bounced hundreds and hundreds of times will finally not bounce any more. The best medicine, taken day in, day out, will no longer be effective. A truth constantly repeated, generation after generation, is eventually disbelieved. That is what has happened all around us. People are no longer moved by fear of death or by the hope of life eternal. All they ask is that death not be mentioned. And thus it seems a conspiracy of silence has descended. We all pretend toward our neighbor that the possibility of his death could never happen. No other rule of behavior is so scrupulously observed as this. The last favor we offer a man on his death-bed is the pretension that his sickness could not possibly be terminal. And if the patient realizes how serious his condition is, he still wants, as a rule, to hear the opposite. Some of you may know the touching tale by a contemporary French author, in which a young widow takes her children every Thursday to visit a distant elderly relative. He has promised to remember her in his last will. One Thursday, they have taken the five-hour trip and found the patient worse. He feels wretched. "Don't you think," he says, "I should make a will? Don't you think you should go and fetch the lawyer?" But she senses the secret fear behind the question. "Don't worry," she replies. "You'll soon be better." And he smiles, reassured. The next day he is dead, without having made his will. His closest relatives get everything. But she can comfort herself with the thought that she gave up everything in order to keep from him the knowledge that he was going to die. She did for him the last act of kindness.

When a man feels the shadow of death upon him and has an urge to speak with his loved ones about it to help him to understand it and face up to it, they stop him from doing so. They play a comedy, pretending that such a prospect is out of the question, keeping up the pretense to the very end. They believe they are doing him a service by persuading him not to think about it. But all they have done is to make him lonely. They have refused to help him.

In this conspiracy of silence, death asserts its rule over modern man. You can see as well as I the unnaturalness of this conspiracy. Let us observe ourselves at this very moment. Look at our involuntary embarrassment. We know each other. We share the thought that we all must die. We know that sooner or later a time will come for us to do the last honors or have someone perform them for us. First, they will stand in the street outside our homes, wearing their black gloves in mourning and chatting with one another, discussing how long we had been sick, what we had died of, which doctor had tended us, whether we had had an easy end or a hard one. And then they will turn to other topics.

Although we feel this strange embarrassment, I yet believe we share an awareness that helps us to overcome the thoughtlessness with which death is usually ignored. It helps us to understand what the apostle meant when he said that in the kingdom of Jesus, the last enemy, death, will be destroyed.

Death still prevails in the outside world and will continue to reign as long as the world lasts. But where men have inwardly overcome it, its rule is at an end. If this is true for us and other modern men, then the word of the apostle is on its way to fulfillment—in another, different, more spiritual way than he probably expected, but to fulfillment all the same.

I would rather not speak here on the church's teaching about the death of Jesus, or to what extent his death is the victory over death. What I am concerned about is the direct teaching which his spirit enacts in us, children of time, if we are serious about it and confident that there really is something of the spirit of Christ in us and that the profound experiences of life are taking effect in us. For surely you all agree with me that experiences exist which we feel to be Christian, events which represent for us the very heart of Christian truth. Because we want to look at the world in a Christian way, those experiences take shape within us. They gain stature not only in ourselves but in those around us who are traveling along the same way.

Let me then say that in our age the spirit of Christ really overcomes death, the last enemy, by helping us to take a calm and natural attitude toward it. This view of death differs greatly from one in which men close their eyes and look away in terror.

The natural contemplation of death can be comforting. Have you ever considered how dreadful it would be if our lives had no appointed end but went on forever? Even a man who has not been hard hit by misfortune in life shudders at the thought that life might never end. Can you imagine that as far as the eye can see into the future we should remain enmeshed in the desires and troubles of this life and that all the ensuing envy, hatred, and malice, our own and other people's, should continue to pile up undiminished?

If you have ever considered how intolerable the burden of life would be without the understood certainty that it has an appointed end, you know that death comes to all, even to the most fortunate, not as an enemy but as a deliverance.

We must all become familiar with the thought of death if we want to grow into really good people. We need not think of it every day or every hour. But when the path of life leads us to some vantage point where the scene around us fades away and we contemplate the distant view right to the end, let us not close our eyes. Let us pause for a moment, look at the distant view, and then carry on.

Thinking about death in this way produces true love for life. When we are familiar with death, we accept each week, each day, as a gift. Only if we are able thus to accept life—bit by bit—does it become precious.

Only familiarity with the though of death creates true, inward freedom from material things. The ambition, greed, and love of power that we keep in our hearts, that shackle us to this life in chains of bondage, cannot in the long run deceive the man who looks death in the face. Rather, by contemplating his end, he eventually feels purified and delivered from his baser self, from material things, and from other men, as well as from fear and hatred of his fellow men.

Often, as we look at ourselves and others, we realize how weak and bad our lives are. This is because we haven't thought of death and therefore have not achieved an inward freedom from life.

But even if a human being has been able to cope with the usual fear of death and even if he has overcome his reluctance to think about it and has looked it straight in the eye, even if he has managed to resign himself to the prospect of death and even if he longs for it with the feeling religious poets have described so movingly—like the apostle Paul who had to fight inwardly against that longing to stop it from becoming too strong—even such a man is still afraid of one thing: The fear of being torn from those who need him.

This fear can never be banned. It sometimes overcomes us like lightning. A man and a woman have not experienced everything together in life unless, looking at each other, they have involuntarily asked the question: What would become of you without me?

A mother has not known the deepest relationship with her child if she has not suddenly been seized by a nameless terror: What would become of my child without me?

For this is the the deepest realization when we try to plumb the depth of life: what holds the deepest meaning in life is not what we hope for, nor what we wish from life, but it is the near and far people who are in need of us.

This same fear overcomes us when we look at those who mean something to us and we ask ourselves in horror: What would our life be like without them?

Face up to this fear, too. Don't push it into the farthest corner of your thoughts. Have the courage to put it into words at the proper time. For something deep and sanctifying takes place when people who belong to each other share the thought that every day, each coming hour, may separate them. In this awareness we always find that the initial anxiety about those who are left behind gives way to another, deeper question: What will happen to that which *was* between us? Have we given each other everything we could? Have we been everything we might have been to one another? Is there anything we would like to undo, something we wish had never happened? This concern then becomes foremost in our minds. We then feel we can bear the parting if we have treated each other with such love. What a different world this would be if men dared to look deeply at each other, if they kept in mind the prospect of being torn from each other. Each would then become sacred to the other because of death.

How can death be overcome? By regarding, in moments of deepest concentration, our lives and those who are part of our lives as though we already had lost them in death, only to receive them back for a little while.

But this is not the ordinary way of looking at death. It is what the apostle Paul is always preaching in his letters as the first and foremost mystery of Christ's religion—that those who belong to the Lord in spirit have shared with him in spiritual experience his death and resurrection to a new life. They now live in this world as men who are inwardly freed from the world by death.

And what about immortality? You may think it strange that I have spoken so much about death and not a word about immortality, the word one generally uses to dispel one's fears. Perhaps one has talked too much and too superficially about immortality, in order to comfort people in face of death. Hence the word has been depreciated. Immortality believed in for the sake of comfort is not genuine immortality. The impression it makes on us is as fleeting as a picture painted on a wall in watercolors—the next shower of rain will wash it away. It is imposed on people from the outside. They soon forget about it, preferring to stifle their fear of death by refusing to think about it.

But the man who dares to live his life with death before his eyes, the man who receives life back bit by bit and lives as though it did not belong to him by right but has been bestowed on him as a gift, the man who has such freedom and peace of mind that he has overcome death in his thoughts—such a man believes in eternal life because it is already his, it is a present experience, and he already benefits from its peace and joy. He cannot describe this experience in words. He may not be able to conform his view with the traditional picture of it. But one thing he knows for certain: Something within us does not pass away, something goes on living and working wherever the kingdom of the spirit is present. It is already working and living within us, because in our hearts we have been able to reach life by overcoming death.

May Paul's words—that in the kingdom of Christ the last enemy, death, has been vanquished—then come true in us. Of course, it has not happened yet. Most people around us still live in bondage to death. They won't mention death's name, and they refuse to think about it. But you, remember, you are called upon to save someone or other from this bondage. When the opportunity arises to say a word that might show him the way, don't hesitate.

{ 10 }

*My Brother's Keeper**

For what shall it profit a man, if he shall gain the whole world, and lose his own soul?   MARK 8:36

W<small>E ARE THINKING</small> today of the young people who have just been confirmed, and I have asked some of them to join us here for a short hour of meditation.

The beginning of our text, which is to form the basis of our thoughts, has a meaning for them very different from the one it has for us. Much of their feeling today finds an echo in the words "gain the whole world." For today has a special meaning not only in their religious life but also in their ordinary everyday existence. Life is opening up before them. It is as though they were standing in a doorway open to freedom, looking out at the whole landscape that lies before them. They have that sense of power peculiar to young people like themselves. They are confident in their own capacities, in what they still want to learn, in their work, in their health. However humble they may feel, they are still convinced that they will win a portion of

* *Preached Palm Sunday, April 4, 1909, at the afternoon service at St. Nicolai's Church.*

77

this world and happiness for themselves. All around them float dreams of advancement and healthy ambition.

I would never want to say anything to dampen this wonderful feeling. I remember how deeply moved I was at my own confirmation. This is how it ought to be. May these youth have a job to do and the ability to do it. May they persevere and have the health to realize the hopes they place in life. And may the hopes we place in them, the new and fresh generation, be fulfilled.

But let them also remember the rest of the text: "For what shall it profit a man, if he shall gain the whole world, and lose his own soul?" Let them make this also a part of their joy in life.

What does the word "soul" mean? Who can say what the soul is? You will meet people who say there is no such thing as a soul. They argue their opinion with sarcasm and scientific learning. No one can give a definition of the soul. But we know what it feels like. The soul is the sense of something higher than ourselves, something that stirs in us thoughts, hopes, and aspirations which go out to the world of goodness, truth, and beauty. The soul is a burning desire to breathe in this world of light and never to lose it —to remain children of light. On this day, in the springtime of your life, when the highest and purest that is in you blossoms forth out of your everyday thoughts like spring flowers, you know what is meant by soul if you listen for it. The excitement and enthusiasm of your inner selves tell you vividly, better than human words are able.

This is something you know. Now one who had more experience in life and knows what may become of it is saying to you: Be on your guard. See that you never lose it. You are not yet aware what it means to "harm the Soul." You can't imagine the feelings of one who has lost his health and must go on living as a cripple. Only one who has endured such despair himself or has lived through it with others knows what it is like. Only he who has known the terrible damage wreaked on his soul or has seen it happen to others knows what it means. A silent agony is brooding over the human race. Many who look outwardly happy are not happy in reality. For they know in their heart of hearts that they have forfeited the right to truth and goodness. They themselves have shut the door to the sacred and pure.

When I was out visiting a few days ago, I called on a woman who wanted to show me something in her attic. As she was about to leave her apartment, she hesitated and went back inside to fetch her key. Then she said, "My door has a lock which cannot be opened from the outside. If I slam it shut, I lock myself out of my own apartment." So it is with people. Through their own conduct they often lock themselves out of the best that is within them. Only afterward do they realize how poor they have become. They have cut themselves off from the world of goodness and beauty within them. They stretch their hands out but do not reach goodness, beauty, and truth. So many people have to bear this burden. It is what makes them lose heart. They pass a garden and know that the flowers blossoming in it are no longer for them. And they know they will never have any real joy in this life. For true joy is like the feeling you young people have now. It means letting the noblest and purest thoughts within you inspire your lives. The purest and most beautiful thoughts *within us* are *only those* which *move* us deeply.

I do not want to frighten you by telling you about the temptations life will bring. Anyone who is healthy in spirit will overcome them. But there is something I want you to realize. It does not matter so much what you do. What matters is whether your soul is harmed by what you do. If your soul is harmed something irreparable happens, the extent of which you won't realize until it will be too late.

And others harm their souls even without being exposed to great temptations. They simply let their souls wither. They allow themselves to be dulled by the joys and worries and distractions of life, not realizing that thoughts which earlier meant a great deal to them in their youth turned into meaningless sounds. In the end they have lost all feeling for everything that makes up the inner life.

You are saying to yourselves now that this can never happen to you. How could all that you feel today within yourselves perish? But it is just this creeping danger I want to warn you about. You know of the disease in Central Africa called sleeping sickness. First its victims get slightly tired. Then the disease gradually intensifies until the afflicted person lies asleep all the time and finally dies from exhaustion. The famous Professor Koch from Berlin visited Africa eighteen months ago to study sleeping sickness. He diagnosed the first symptoms of this malady in many people who only laughed at him and told him they felt perfectly well. Yet he was quite certain that they had already been infected, and he was distraught about their refusal to undergo treatment.

There also exists a sleeping sickness of the soul. Its most dangerous aspect is that one is unaware of its coming. That is why you have to be careful. As soon as you notice the slightest sign of indifference, the moment you become aware of the loss of a certain seriousness, of longing, of enthusiasm and zest, take it as a warning. You should realize that your soul has suffered harm.

Your soul suffers if you live superficially. People need times in which to concentrate, when they can search their inmost selves. It is tragic that most men have not achieved this feeling of self-awareness. And finally, when they hear the inner voice they do not want to listen anymore. They carry on as before so as not to be constantly reminded of what they have lost. But as for you, resolve to keep a quiet time both in your homes and here within these peaceful walls when the bells ring on Sundays. Then your souls can speak to you without being drowned out by the hustle and bustle of everyday life.

And persevere in action. You cannot imagine how important action is for the inner life. What kind of man is he who is not active, who does not apply his ability and energy to help where help is needed?

The interior joy we feel when we have done a good deed, when we feel we have been needed somewhere and have lent a helping hand, is the nourishment the soul requires. Without those times when man feels himself to be part of the spiritual world by his actions, his soul decays. So many drift into the misery of indifference because they did not start out with the vital power that comes from helping others. Don't forget this. Start right now, keep your eyes open, become active in the kingdom of God.

{ 11 }

Be True to Yourself[*]

*Be thou faithful unto death, and I will give thee a
crown of life.* REVELATION 2:10

THIS IS THE LAST time I will have the privilege of preaching to you at the afternoon service. These Sunday after-
noons have been some of the most wonderful experiences
of my life. You must often have noticed in the last few
years that only with some effort and by applying my utmost
strength was I able to talk to you. Often, as I stepped down
from the pulpit, I had the impression that you were all
very generous and understanding with me. Yet all the
exhaustion of these hours was nothing compared to my
knowledge of being one with you, of being uplifted together. Our paths are outwardly diverging, but we are
inwardly united. So we must look for a central point from
which to observe at this moment the far-off horizon. We do
not ask what we wish for each other, or how we should
provide together for what lies in the future. No, together
we ask: What makes us feel certain that we are doing in

* *Preached Sunday, February 25, 1912, at the afternoon service at St.
Nicolai's Church.*

this life what we ought to do? What gives us satisfaction?
Now you will see the point of my text, "Be faithful," and
how it will serve as the focus for our last meditation together.

There is a great expanse before us: "Faithful unto
death." That means to the very end of our life, be it sooner
or later. And the sun shines over it gloriously: "I will give
you the crown of life."

I cannot define what "faithful" means. The real meaning
begins at the point at which verbal explanation is in-
adequate and ceases to be. Yet we know in our inner heart
what it is trying to say. All the good we may recognize
or desire is nothing in itself and leads nowhere unless it is
strengthened in the thought of faithfulness. It is just like
the hardening of metal. No one can explain how it happens.
First it is weak and pliable, but then it becomes a hundred
times as strong as it was before. Nor can we explain how
every human virtue only achieves strength and fulfillment
after it has been hardened on the anvil of faithfulness.

I have seen rivers carrying boulders along, where the
banks were breached and the fields and meadows were
covered with sand and laid desolate. Thus it is with men
when they are unfaithful, when they are not kept on course
by an inner power. Nothing prevents them from swerving
off their course and destroying their surroundings through
carelessness or temper or fear—an act they ought not to
have done, an event which brings no blessing. Faithfulness
is the inner power of life which enables us to understand
ourselves. As you observe other people, you will see how
few of them are faithful. And yet, as we look at the few
who are, it makes us yearn to become faithful as they are.
For faithfulness, a melody composed in our youth, can be
overpowered by the discords of carelessness and by the
jangling cynicism which says: That's just the way of the

world: nobody can be faithful in this life in all his actions.

First our text says: "Be true to yourself." This is not just a romantic phrase: true to yourself. For you know it is something compelling that takes place within and repeats itself again and again. Each act of unfaithfulness toward our inner being is a blot on our souls. If we continue to be unfaithful, our souls are eventually torn apart and we slowly bleed to death. Harmony and strength exist in our lives only when our outer selves match our inner selves, when this great truthfulness forges an inner harmony between our deepest and purest yearnings and the goals we pursue in life.

True to ourselves and true also in our relations with other people. A well-known maxim says: "Be true to men as they are true to you." Thus the way other people treat us determines our own degree of faithfulness. This saying asks us: Why do you treat them differently from the way they treat you? Pay other people back in our own coin! And yet, woe betide us if we listen to this voice! For the voice *within* us says: To be faithful means to be inwardly united with others in a relationship that puts us above all trivialities of daily life. We become aware that the noble understanding we are privileged to share in rare moments will always unite us closer than anything else. Being true to others also means the realization of responsibility in every detail toward others, be they friends or strangers. The first pages of Holy Scripture contain a dreadful saying which men use as an excuse for themselves: "Am I my brother's keeper?" This question, with its implication of irresponsibility, permeates the whole history of mankind and the life of each of us. Each of us has to take issue with such reasoning as: My horizon is limited. So-and-so is no concern of mine. I can take no responsibility for him. How cleverly a man tries to pass this off as logic! But in his heart, faithfulness says: That is not true. We are obligated to do everything we can for others, for friends and strangers alike. Jesus impressed this upon us, in his moving way, when he said that everyone who needs us is our neighbor. Everything we do for anyone is also done for *Jesus* and will receive its blessing from him. Such utter faithfulness does not make our lives easier. Far from it; such profound faithfulness makes our lives difficult. It lays heavy responsibility upon us. It makes us troubled when reason would prefer to be left in peace. From this commitment let us act to friend and stranger alike.

Being faithful in our calling does not simply mean being outwardly faithful in fulfilling our duties, but faithful in everything that we can accomplish here on earth. Faithful in that highest sense of awareness that we ourselves are not masters of our own ability and knowledge. They, like our talents and our health, are a loan presented for our use. We must live as people who know that such temporary possessions are not true belongings and that we must give account for our management of them. We shall be asked how we have handled these valuable loans. We must not live our lives like men who say: "This and this is mine. I can help myself to anything I need to make me happy and give me pleasure." No, we must live like men who know and are becoming ever more mature in the knowledge that the most precious gift in life is to live not for ourselves but for the benefit of others, for truth and goodness.

Finally, be true to Jesus and his spirit. For Jesus' spirit is the secret of true life. It teaches us what life demands from us. We are his disciples, not because we are immune to human frailty but because we must serve him. And we have to serve him because he lives among us, because he spiritually cares for us and suffers for our times. We serve him because he seeks men and shows them how to do his will, men who will obey him in things both great and small.

This faithfulness toward Jesus is not a sort of complicated, mystical notion that sounds quite impressive in sermons but has no meaning in practical life. Far from it. Whoever has looked into the eyes of Jesus as he appears to us in his words knows that true happiness consists of service to this great One and his Spirit—and a life offered to his work. Those who accept this mode of life, who know how to live it, become brothers and sisters.

Our text goes on to say, "I will give you a crown of life." The crown of life is not a jeweled diadem to be pressed with honors upon our brow. When this life will be over, when something new will begin, we do not know. We only know that the crown of life is worn here and now by the faithful. It is worn inwardly in the peace and joy that come from being faithful, and it is expressed outwardly in the glory which fills our lives. Obviously anything may happen to us outwardly, and life may bring many hardships. And yet—our joy is on a higher level, unaffected by our outward lot. For our joy lies in the awareness that we are faithful in our inmost hearts. Thus we maintain our spiritual communion with Jesus and his eternal spirit, and this presence brings holiness and peace along our way.

I walked on one of these late summer days along the beautiful roads of Lorraine. The view was endless. One range of hills rose behind another. The sun was setting before me, casting its gold over the whole landscape. Even the trees on the distant hills seemed afire. The glow surrounded me and gave me a wonderful feeling. The whole scene was a parable of human life. In our inner faithfulness toward ourselves, in our inner contact with the incomprehensible, with infinity, we approach life's sunset, bathed more and more in light until the final moment when the earthly sun sets for us. Even if the outward sun goes down for us, too! How does that wonderful hymn put it?

> Where are you, Sun?
> Night chased you.
> Night is the foe of day,
> But Jesus, my bliss,
> You are the Sun of my heart.
> You penetrate my heart with your radiance.

And what the hymn says of earthly night can be said equally of the darkness found in every life, of all the toil and sadness that it brings. Such darkness cannot extinguish the light of earthly joy. The darker it gets, the more brilliantly shines the sun of joy in our unity and in our inward confirmation with the spirit of Jesus. For he came into the world and became our Savior. He has lifted us up with his great spirit from our fears and trivialities, from our anxiety. He has directed our eyes toward the truth, toward the infinite spirit within us which longs for eternity. Because of our faith in this life and beyond, we know the quietude of the peace that passes all understanding.

{ 12 }

The Peace of God*

*And the peace of God, which passeth all understanding,
shall keep your hearts and minds through Christ Jesus.*

PHILIPPIANS 4:7

THIS TEXT has been read on many Sundays, as we were
leaving this gathering. It has often guided us through the
week. Let it be heard once more this Sunday, as I prepare
to part with you, knowing we shall not meet again for a
long time.

I had chosen it as the word of blessing because it expresses what I have sought to preach to you as the gospel
and verbalizes the communion of thought that should exist
between us.

Our text places two things side by side: "the peace of
God" and "understanding," or reason. They are not op-
posites but complementary truths. A path should lead
from the one to the other, and peace and understanding
should be linked together in each of us.

---

* *Preached Sunday, March 9, 1913, at the morning service at St.
Nicolai's Church, Schweitzer's farewell sermon before leaving for
Lambaréné.*

In our age, reason is belittled and slighted—in Catholic and Protestant churches alike. People seem to think such irreverence will make religion easier. In this age I have come before you, daring to speak of religion with joy and reverence. I have tried to use reason to illuminate everything that concerns faith and religion, for I know from personal experience that *this* is the way my own religion has been kept alive and deepened. The more I understood Jesus, the clearer it became to me and the more I was impressed by the way he combined faith and simple common sense. The more I studied the history of Christianity, the more I realized the extent of the errors and disagreements which started because men from the first generation to this day played up faith and piety at the expense of reason, and so put asunder what God had joined together harmoniously.

As you know, reason in this connotation does not simply mean ordinary, superficial reflection. It means the light of the spirit which shines from within and tries to throw its beam of comprehension on the world and all that is in it—the enigma of existence, the purpose and destiny of human life—as it searches out a path for us. There can be only one path, the path to peace and harmony between all of us and toward every event and in all that exists, whether visible or invisible. The path to peace is renewed in joy and in sorrow, in work and in suffering. As we stand in the world, bound with a thousand bonds, we gradually can shake off the effects of its powerful shackles only if we achieve inward freedom, knowing that, come what may, worldly chains will have no power over us.

The peace of God which passeth all understanding. It is like distant snowy caps of mountains gleaming in the sun. They stand above the mist and appear to rise abruptly, whereas actually beneath them are the lower-lying hills which they crown, and nobody can reach the higher levels without first climbing the foothills. Human understanding and the peace of God are similarly related. Many people in our time are irreligious, not because their faith has been destroyed but because they have not been led far enough on the path of reason—to the very end, to where the path of peace continues beyond reason. They have not given themselves to constant reflection about the world, the future of the nations, or the utter enigma of their own existence. They have not used reason to purify and solidify their religious inheritance. They have never appropriated the eternal truth enshrined within religion. Instead, they let it fall by the wayside as they passed through life.

However much opinions and expressions of times may change, whether they be presented by the prophets or Jesus or the Reformers, the person who thinks things through to their logical conclusion gains eternal insights into life. These insights may become in each of us again a living truth.

It is reason which helps to get beyond the trivialities of our daily life. We become concerned about all that is happening, with all the questions that beset our times. It makes us participate in this world and feel personally what is happening on earth. This experience can be achieved equally by the educated and the uneducated. There are some famous sages who have never really applied their minds or had any real awareness of life. Craftsmen who have seldom left their workshops have yet had a strong urge to comprehend things and to experience them. Only he who knows this, in one way or another, has an ever-increasing desire for peace.

Many people in this world have never really known this yearning or, if they have ever known it, have lost it. They have reached the point when they say: This is the life I desire; I will arrange it like this to suit myself; this is my aim, and I am satisfied. People who feel this way have allowed the light of reason, which could radiate from them and light up everything, to grow dim. They only experience the trivialities of immediate concern and have ceased to care about everything that happens. So they fix up for themselves a small, shallow corner of private happiness and seek in it their enjoyment. But those who keep the light of common sense alive within them, and use it to keep in touch with life and all its problems, will be led to an increasing awareness that our happiness or unhappiness is not determined by what happens to us in everyday life. However favorable our circumstances, however successful our enterprises, however much envied we are by our fellow men, we still may not be happy. For peace alone is the source of happiness. The more our reasoning throws us into the turmoil of life's problems, the more we yearn for peace. We are led up the mountains until the glaciers begin to glitter before us. Then reasoning bids us climb still higher, still further into the light, still further into peace and quietude.

All attempts to acquire knowledge teach us finally that behind all things and all deeds is an unfathomable will. In external events a universal will springs from the source of life, communicating itself to all things, containing all that is. It is the will of God. Within ourselves is our own will, somehow stemming from his will, rooted in it and yet our very own. The ultimate questions of our life transcend knowledge. One riddle after another surrounds us. But the final question of our being has but one concern, and it decides our fate. Again and again we are thrown back to it. What will become of our own will? How does it find itself in the will of God? The highest insight man can attain is the yearning for peace, for the union of his will with an infinite will, his human will with God's will. Such a will does not cut itself off and live in isolation like a puddle that is bound to dry up when the heat of summer comes. No, it is like a mountain stream, relentlessly splashing its way to the river, there to be swept on to the limitless ocean.

Mark well, the apostle does not speak of faith that is higher than all reason. He rather says the peace of God. Reason never complacently rests in faith, for true peace comes from what happens with our own will, from what it seeks. The peace of God can be ours only if our will finds peace in the infinite.

People often think that for our will to find rest in God's means a fatalistic resignation to the will of God. But frequently the passive will of such people finds this impossible because their active will has not found its way into God's will. How can they find the way by night if they haven't looked for it by day?

Active people search for the way to the peace of God while it is yet light. Only in the light can our feet step firmly upon the path. Illumination enables us to persevere along the path even though suffering lies in the way. We must not allow ourselves to be overwhelmed by misfortune's treacherous blows. We must not wait until we are evicted from a life of comfort and are suddenly reminded that a will exists outside of us, a will stronger than ours, with which we have to come to terms.

Before suffering drives us to pray, "Thy will be done on earth as it is in heaven," we should pray for it as men of will and action, and shall find the joy of our life in such prayer. This inner feeling of God's will within us, with us, around us, and with the whole world must fill our lives and our being. Then we shall share the hopes and anxieties of others and help them as best we can, that

God's will may be done around us. We shall all work in his kingdom and find our fulfillment in it, happier in our daily work, however uninteresting and monotonous it may be. For then we shall know that we can bring the spirit of the kingdom of God into life, wherever we happen to be. Then, too, every person will find some voluntary occupation in which to serve God.

When our wills are united with the will of God, we never take all the goodness and beauty and people and things in life for granted, but we accept them again and again as a gift from him—given that we may serve him with still greater joy and thank him for it.

Thus our active will must search for the peace of God. Those who travel this path and have experienced the peace of God can face all eventualities. The passive will is then bound to obey the will of God. They may still find suffering trying and difficult to explain. But an inner motivation will carry them up from that low point of despair where others remain resigned. They have gathered up a treasure in their hearts—the peace of God. His peace will support them until their soul is calm again. Life does not take them unawares. They have prepared themselves beforehand for everything that might befall them, and they have received it from the Lord. In the hour of trial, what they have to face, be it the loss of health, beloved ones, or happiness, the saying "The Lord gave, the Lord hath taken away, blessed be the name of the Lord" is for them no empty phrase. For they have taken to heart the opening words: "The Lord gave." And so they are prepared for the day when they will have to learn the rest of the text.

Where the active and the passive will seek for the peace of God, our hearts and minds will be preserved in Christ Jesus, our Lord. Then we shall share the knowledge—and realize it more and more—that he is our Master.

Then we shall feel the pure and life-giving breath of his spirit and be united in him with one another.

On many a Sunday I have given the blessing with this text, aware of my great privilege as inexpressible happiness to preach the gospel to you. I have always felt the words as a moment of silent meditation shared together before we went out into another week. We seemed to seek together the peace of God, the union of our wills with his. That has been our highest aim, whether we were still active or had to be passive. As we have shared these thoughts together in such blessed moments we have all gained strength and courage for everything we might encounter in the week ahead.

May this hour unite us once more, so we know with each other and from each other the only one joy in life, the joy of which all other pleasures are but a reflection, the only joy capable of lightening our deepest misery: the peace of God which passeth all understanding, the union of our poor mortal wills with his will in deed and joy and sorrow, and that we shall pursue this peace together, for we shall then become ever richer and stronger in it, and able to show others the way.

{ 13 }

The Future of Mankind*

And the peace of God, which passeth all understanding, shall keep your hearts and minds through Christ Jesus.

PHILIPPIANS 4:7

YEARS HAVE PASSED since I last had the privilege of speaking to you within the walls of this church. How I longed every Sunday for the moment when I would be allowed to be with you once more! How homesick I have felt for this place! I could almost hear the bells ringing, calling you to church. I nearly felt that I was with you although oceans separated us. Now my dreams have been fulfilled— in these agonizing, critical days when our destinies are about to be decided, when the future that lies before us seems darker than ever before.

Now I stand before you and I think of the sorrow and the suffering which have befallen every one of you. I remember those choirboys who sang the chorale so beautifully from the organ loft when I said farewell to you. Many

* Preached Sunday, October 13, 1918, at St. Nicolai's Church, Schweitzer's first sermon after his return from Lambaréné and the internment camp of St. Rémy de Provence.

have since died as men and are buried in distant lands. You have all experienced severe privations. You have all lost loved ones. Many of you have seen the utter ruin of your life's work. Others have labored to create a better future for their children, but the children are no longer with us. Yet others have had to sacrifice sons on whose support they counted for their old age.

Where shall I direct your thoughts in this hour that we may together turn sorrow, pain, and distress into peace of mind? I will give you the blessing—the peace of God which passeth all understanding. With this word I parted from you. With this word I come before you on my return.

What is the peace of God? The silence of our will in his infinite will.

How is this surrender to the will of God achieved? Should God's will be a thought placed before us to gaze at until we are fascinated and hypnotized by it? I dare not suggest this to you, for I do not know if it will lead us to the true peace of God. It always seems to me a counsel of despair when people try to persuade themselves that God is to blame for everything. They do violence to their own thoughts, refuse to take a sane, commonsense view of things, and lose their energy. They possess peace because something within them broke.

Nor it is helpful to try to see the will of God in every event, whether it be the fate of individuals or of a nation or of all mankind. True, when we look back, we may understand much that was inexplicable to us at the time. In retrospect, we see how good came out of evil, meaning out of senselessness. By the same token, when the thinking human being contemplates the past, the discoveries we made in the course of life are often mysterious. When viewed from the valley immediately below, mountains seem chaotic, but when observed from the distant plains they appear as an orderly range of peaks. But alongside of this, still a good deal remains in our private lives as well as in public events in which the senseless has not acquired meaning, nor the evil turned out to be a blessing in disguise.

Anyone who tries to explain why a mother should lose her son, why a friend will betray his friend, why a cliché phrase may triumph over truth, will get lost in a maze. We will never comprehend why the infinite will, in order to realize its completion, requires the incomplete, or how evil can result in good. This riddle forces itself on us over and over again. Many unanswered questions remain. No forced attempt to reason out these events can give us the peace of God. There is a different way, a way born from inward experience. We may not have been given the privilege of understanding how events are expressing the will of God. But one thing we do know, and on that knowledge all else depends—the will of God is directed only toward one thing: the spiritual.

The primary insight is man's awareness that his destiny is not synonymous with his daily experiences. You who have been through so much suffering have tasted this inner freedom from outward events. You know there have been times when, according to the rules, you should have been smashed to the ground by what occurred. In such moments you were surprised by yourselves. You had the feeling you were being lifted up inwardly, as though the spiritual were triumphing over the material. You recognized a sort of happiness—if it can be called that—a happiness which would have been hidden by an unbroken succession of good days. You began to understand what the apostle Paul meant when he said, "Though our outward man perish, yet the inward man is renewed day by day." The peace of

God begins when this fleeting experience can be preserved and turned into a permanent conviction.

The peace of God is pulsating power, not quietude. The knowledge we must reach lies on the heights where knowledge and obedience coalesce and become one. The question is not: How can I explain the events that occur? You should ask rather: What can I make out of them? That is the profound understanding for which we must struggle. Two people have similar experiences. One remains unchanged, while the other grows spiritually because he discovers there is meaning in events.

The basic significance of all difficulty is that it reorients us from the external to the spiritual. The meaning and purpose of the world remain to a large extent inexplicable. But one thing is clear: the purpose of all events is spiritual. The purpose of existence is that we human beings, all nations and the whole of humanity, should constantly progress toward perfection. We must search for these conditions and hold fast to these ideals. If we do this, our finite spirit will be in harmony with the infinite. If we have this yearning, we shall attain to the peace of God.

Events are like mountains and hills that divert the river from its straight course, forcing it to twist and turn yet leading it in the right direction. Were it not for these obstructions, the river would get lost in the countryside and miss the way to the sea, toward which it is straining to go. And just as the individual must identify himself with the spiritual aims of the infinite Spirit if he wants events to help him grow in experience, so too must nations. As we, if we are to find peace, must have faith in the spiritual future of our own nation, so too must we have faith in the spiritual future of all mankind. Some progress must come; a race of men must arise to form nations united by spiritual goals, attempting the highest that can be achieved on earth. I mean by this something much more than those who hold speeches in Parliament and such ventures as they talk about in the League of Nations.

The tragedy of our times is that the ideals we need are made superficial and profane. Too frequently, ideals are degraded into propaganda clichés which serve as a perfect excuse for situations far from ideal. This has nothing to do with what we as religious people are thinking. For what *we* are thinking about is what our Lord called "the kingdom of God," something arising naturally from the ever-ennobled thought of men. In the hideous chaos which humanity presents today, we must still believe, all appearances to the contrary, that eventually a race of men united by common ideals will come into being.

Truly the events that have happened so rapidly in the field of human relations now easily divert us from the way to the kingdom of God. Such hurdles, which formerly did not exist, must be cleared away. But if in the hearts of enough people the conviction arises—and convinced they must become—our troubles will be overcome. Nothing can defeat the spirit when it comes in purity and power.

Years ago, when I preached my farewell sermon on the kingdom of God, the clouds were already gathering for the storm. I spoke to you then of the bell from the cathedral, which tolled every evening over our town. It seemed to ring its message over all the land: "Thy kingdom come!" and it summoned us day by day to collect our thoughts for a few moments. That bell is now silenced. Will it ever peal again? But within our hearts it will ring out the same message from all the tribulation we have suffered: "Thy kingdom come!" We have buried our loved ones and our hopes. More has been asked of us than of any other generation. But out of the destruction we have suffered, we must preserve as the most precious ideal for the new age our faith in the future of mankind. Ours is the responsibility of transferring this faith to the coming generation. The sun of hope is not shining upon our paths. Night is still here, and our generation will not live to see the dawn of the new day. But if we have preserved our faith in that which must come, then stars will lighten our way and bring Light. Peace of God, fill our hearts, help us.

{ 14 }

*Sacrifice of Others**

And God shall wipe away all tears from their eyes; and there shall be no more death, neither sorrow, nor crying, neither shall there be any more pain: for the former things are passed away. REVELATION 21:4

For the fifth time in this season in which autumn fades into winter, we are remembering the dead. We remember those who have died of old age, sickness, or accident, but we also commemorate the loss of those fallen at the hands of men in this murderous war.

How did they die? When the bullet tore into their bodies, they bled to death. They were trapped in barbed wire and hung there for days, famished and crying for help, and no one was able to came to their aid. They froze to death at night upon the cold earth. Mines buried them or blew them to bits in midair. The gurgling currents took its toll of ships in which they sailed. They fought the waves until they were exhausted or braced themselves against the walls of the ship's hold in helpless

* *Preached Sunday, December 1, 1918, at a memorial service for the dead of World War I, held at St. Nicolai's Church.*

panic. Those who survived injuries on the battlefield or in the water perished after suffering agonies for weeks or months in field hospitals, struggling even to go on living the life of a cripple. During those tense months, when darkness and silence enshrouded us, did we not seem to hear a crying and a wailing arising from earth to heaven? We tried to shut it out, but to no avail. It went on echoing in our ears.

Now all this woe belongs to the past. Suffering is ended for those who were wounded or killed by human hands. God has wiped away all tears from their eyes. There is no more sorrow or sighing or pain for them.

How shall we celebrate their memory? Have you ever followed the coffin of one who was part of your life and made a sudden resolution to unite yourself with the departed one by vowing that from that moment on you would do something or give up something in memory of him? I believe that is what we men of all nations must do now. We must promise to vow for those who fell in the war.

Let us first make the simplest and most natural resolution—that we will not forget them or what their death means. Do not think that this will be easy. Time blots out memories we would like to cherish, and takes them away if we do not defend ourselves against it. I already dread the day when women who have lost their husbands in battle will no longer be given the sympathy and honor they deserve, when orphans who lost their fathers will no longer find the love and protection they need. Already we are failing to do or say enough for those who are left behind. But you guard against indifference. The bereaved are a holy inheritance for us. They must feel that we are sensitive to the debt we owe to those who died on the battlefield, that we are trying to work off our debt to the dead by the treatment we show to their survivors.

The crowns and wreaths with which we adorn their graves will express this concern. No storm shall blow them away, no rain make them fade. You may be sure that hundreds and thousands will wound the bereaved with their brutality and lack of compassion. But you must make up for that by *your* compassion.

What else shall we vow for the dead? That they have not died in vain. They gave their lives in every land to save their countrymen from the horror of war and to preserve their liberty. Every nation must realize how grateful it should be to its dead for this. For those nations who were granted victory, the meaning of the deaths of their sons is expressed by the jubilation which reechoes over their graves. For the vanquished, the dead are remembered in sorrow. Outward circumstance decided that the deaths of some were sealed with victory while others were without success. But that is not the final meaning of their deaths. Now that we can look back at the war as a thing of the past, those who made the supreme sacrifice appear as a single army. Differences in uniform or nationality have disappeared. They are men united in pain and suffering. They all present us with a challenge.

For our sins they were delivered up. It was too easy in all nations to think of individual well-being or pain. Human life, that mysterious, irreplaceable treasure, was rated too low. People too glibly spoke of war and the misery it brings. We got used to risking a certain number of human lives, and we glorified our inhumanity in song. When the inevitable came, it was a thousand times more cruel than any of us had imagined. It was so ugly and horrible that we can no longer glorify it. Only suffering and terror remain.

Disregarding all barriers of nationality we remember today those human beings who were sacrificed to the spirit of heartless cruelty. We humiliate ourselves before these dead, and we promise that the heartless spirit in which they were sacrificed shall be destroyed. The frame of mind in which this generation grew up must be destroyed, for the enormity of its sinfulness caused the suffering of the world. We shall teach our children what we have learned and leave to them, as our legacy, the commandment "Thou shalt not kill," for we now know its meaning has far deeper relevance than our teachers and we ourselves ever dreamed of. Those millions who were made to kill, forced to do it in self-defense or under military orders, must impress the horror of what they had to endure on all future generations so that none will ever expose itself to such fate again.

Reverence for human suffering and human life, for the smallest and most insignificant, must be the inviolable law to rule the world from now on. In so doing, we do not replace old slogans with new ones and imagine that some good may come out of high-sounding speeches and pronouncements. We must recognize that only a deep-seated change of heart, spreading from one man to another, can achieve such a thing in this world. The fallen were sacrificed because of a frame of mind that had not yet understood the meaning of the commandment "Thou shalt not kill," the dead have made atonement for our guilt. Their suffering has taken our guilt from us, so that a new age may come and we may work for it.

The paths into which God leads mankind are shrouded in darkness for us. There are only two ground rules. They go together, and each taken by itself is enigmatic. The first is that all sin requires atonement. The second is that all progress demands sacrifice, which has to be paid for by the lives of those chosen to be offered up. We sense this more than we understand it. Sacrifice, like many laws of nature, remains something terrible, but we must submit to it. As children in a powerful age we understand the mysterious element in Holy Scripture better than generations before us did. And above all, it is the obscure thought of the apostle Paul which illuminates it for us. In a word of prophecy he tells us that not only did Christ have to suffer but that his innocent suffering and death must continue in mankind so that the kingdom of God may come. What men in ordinary times cannot understand has been opened up for us. Before our very eyes, God permitted millions to suffer and die innocently. As the disciples recognized that the Lord's death signified the emergence of something new in this world, so we too know it as we look on our dead and mourn. And the power of his sacrifice must be matched by the power of this new order in the world, the new structure we must build.

If you listen you will hear the sound of the kingdom of God in the air as no generation ever could before. We are called upon to take the step which until now has never been possible for man. We have no alternative: the dead are helping us and forcing us to take it. There will be no more sorrow, or crying, or pain, for the former things are passed away. The "former things" is the world without reverence for human life, a world which has excluded itself from the love of God and placed itself under the yoke of misery that man can bring upon fellow man. The present thing is the kingdom of God, for which Jesus died. Millions in the past few months have also died for the new kingdom. They will have died in vain if we remain a generation that hears yet does not hear, sees yet does not see.

Just one more point. We who have survived—either because we have been miraculously saved from a hundred perils or because our destiny has spared us from having to face death and destruction as the othes did—we must not take our good fortune for granted. We cannot simply regard ourselves as men who have risen again from the dead. God in his grace has given us life anew so that we may use it anew. Paul often makes this point. He says that we Christians must look upon ourselves as men who have died in Christ and have risen with him to a new existence, to walk henceforth in newness of life. We should understand this thought better than anyone. How true it must ring for the millions among us who have walked with death in the past years! Now, when we see the sun, we are amazed that we are still alive, amazed that tomorrow the familiar specter of death will no longer be there to threaten us.

The revelations of the Old and New Testaments which speak of the coming of the kingdom of God at the end of time say that Christ will establish it, surrounded and supported by the myriads who have been raised from the dead. If there is any explanation for these mysteries, let me boldly apply them to these times, to us, to the multitudes who have come through death to life again. All the misery we have experienced, all the sorrow and death we have witnessed, all the atrocities we were forced to inflict on one another, have prepared us as no generation ever was prepared before to grasp the dreadful seriousness of things. Our thoughts can give shape to the new age, an age like the kingdom of God. And with clean hands we can work as new people to bring about that which is unavoidably to come.

When I meet acquaintances returning from the front, I often observe a changed expression in their faces, as though the atrocities they witnessed have left an indelible mark on their features. It seems that the horizon of their thoughts have widened further ahead than ever before. This gives me a sense of hope, a faint one perhaps, of a new, deepened, and purified humanity. Is this the harbinger of great things to come? Or will it wither again when the thoughtlessness of daily routine returns or when the distractions of life divert our minds? God protect us from that! It will depend on us who have survived whether those who died for human progress and the kingdom of God died in vain, or whether their suffering and death will bear fruit. If we fail, no other generation for centuries to come can fulfill this promise. That is why we *must* promise, before God and Jesus, to answer the call of duty. Do not be misled if many around you fail to understand the signs of the times and become involved in trivialities. If only we think and do what must be thought and done, a blessing will be given to the world.

This is the way we must remember the dead.

{ 15 }

*Reverence for Life**

*And one of the scribes came, and having heard them rea-
soning together, and perceiving that he had answered
them well, asked him, Which is the first commandment
of all? And Jesus answered him, The first of all the
commandments is, Hear, O Israel; The Lord our God
is one Lord: And thou shalt love the Lord thy God with
all thy heart, and with all thy soul, and with all thy
mind, and with all thy strength: this is the first commandment. And the second is like, namely this, Thou
shalt love thy neighbour as thyself. There is none other
commandment greater than these. And the scribe said
unto him, Well, Master, thou hast said the truth: for
there is one God; and there is none other but he: And
to love him with all the heart, and with all the understanding, and with all the soul, and with all the
strength, and to love his neighbour as himself, is more
than all whole burnt offerings and sacrifices. And when
Jesus saw that he answered discreetly, he said unto him,*

* *Preached Sunday, February 16, 1919, at the morning service at St.
Nicolai's Church.*

Thou art not far from the kingdom of God. And no man after that durst ask him any question.

MARK *12:28–34*

THE SCRIBE WHO ASKS Jesus which commandment is the greatest is in search of knowledge. He wants information about a matter that concerns him, as it does many of his compatriots. In St. Matthew's Gospel, Chapter 22, the scribes pose this question to Jesus in order to tempt him. But the evangelist Mark surely has a better memory when he describes the sympathetic scene in which Jesus and the scribe for one moment have mutual understanding and look into one another's hearts, and then to go their separate ways.

In those days Israelite thinkers used to discuss the possibility of tracing all the commandments, both great and small, back to a single basic law. We, too, have a similar need. What is intrinsic good? I have read to you the eternal sayings of our Lord about forgiveness, mercy, love, and all the other characteristics that we as his disciples should act upon in the world. But we all seem to feel that these are only separate colors broken down from the whitelight of a basic ethical attitude which he requires from us.

Let me ponder this question with you now: What exactly is this basic ethical attitude? Later I will devote several meditations to questions on Christian ethics about which I have been thinking in far-off lands, in the loneliness of the jungle, always with these services here at St. Nicolai's in mind and in the confident hope that someday I might be permitted to speak to you about them.

The question of the basic ethical attitude is uppermost

in our minds nowadays. We are forced to a recognition that previous generations and even we ourselves until recently refused to accept. Now we cannot escape it if we would be truthful: the Christian ethic has never become a power in the world. It has not sunk deep into the minds of men. It has been accepted only superficially, acknowledged in theory more than put into practice. Mankind behaves as if the teaching of Jesus did not exist, as if Christian behavior had no ethical principles at all.

Therefore, constantly repeating the ethical teaching of Jesus is of no use, nor is expounding it is though it were bound to win universal acceptance in the end. It is like trying to paint a wet wall with pretty colors. We first have to create a foundation for the understanding of the teaching and guide our world to a frame of mind in which the teachings of Jesus have meaning. It is by no means easy to interpret Jesus' teachings so as to make them practical to daily life. Let us take as an example the sayings about the greatest of the commandments. What does it mean to love God with all our heart and to do good only out of love for him? Follow up this train of thought and a whole world of new ideas will open. When in life have you chosen to do good out of love for God when you might otherwise have chosen to do evil?

Or take the other commandment: "Love thy neighbour as thyself." Truly, it is wonderful. I could give you the most alluring illustrations to prove it. But can it be done? Suppose you make a resolution to obey it literally, starting tomorrow. What would be the result in a few days?

This is the greatest riddle in Christian ethics. We cannot apply Jesus' teachings directly to our lives, however holy our desire to serve him. Our frustration then leads us to the great danger of making a reverent bow toward Jesus' words, praising them as the "ideal," but in reality leaving them unheeded.

Still another misunderstanding endangers the realization of Christian morality. A certain ethical attitude can easily make us arrogant. If we forgive our enemies, we think we are being virtuous. If we help a man who needs our assistance, we consider ourselves very noble indeed. We perform small acts of goodness possibly in the name of Christ, considering our deeds somehow different and better than those of other men. Thus we acquire a superior and complacent attitude which actually makes us more unethical than those who do not acknowledge the commandments of Jesus or try to live up to them. The demands of Jesus are difficult just because they require us to do something extraordinary. At the same time he asks us to regard these as something usual, ordinary. While the unusual is exactly what he demands of us. For he says that we should regard ourselves as unprofitable servants, however much we may have accomplished.

So there you have it. Now you know why we must think together about the intrinsic good. We want to learn to understand how the exalted demands of Jesus can be carried out in daily life. We wish to take them as the natural duty of man although they are so exalted in fact.

We want to grasp the underlying principle of all ethics and use that principle as the supreme law from which all ethical actions can be derived. Yes, but can morality be grasped at all? Is it not a matter of the heart? Does it not rest upon love? This we have been told again and again for two thousand years. And what is the result?

Let us study men around us both collectively and individually. Why are they so often unstable? Why are even the most devout among them, and often the pious in particular, capable of being swept by prejudice and passions of nationalism into judgments and courses of action entirely void of ethical truth? Because they lack an ethic based on reason and rooted in logic. Because they do not regard ethics as a natural endowment or as part of their faculty of reason.

Reason and heart must act together if a true morality is to be established. Herein lies the real problem for abstract ethics as well as for practical decisions of daily life.

The reason of which I speak penetrates the heart of the matter and embraces the whole of reality, including the realm of the will.

We experience a strange duality when we seek self-understanding in the light of the ethical will within us. On the one hand, we notice its connection with reason. On the other hand, we are forced into decisions that are not rational in ordinary terms but are expressions of demands that would normally be considered extravagant. In this duality, in this strange tension, lies the essence of ethics. We need not fear that an ethic based on reason is geared too low, that it may be too detached and heartless. For when reason really reaches the core of the matter it ceases to be cold reason, whether it wants to or not, and begins to speak with the melody of the heart. And the heart, when it tries to fathom itself, discovers that its realm overlaps the realm of reason. It has to pass through the land of reason to reach the furthest boundary of its own superfluous sphere. How can that be?

Let us explore the basic principle of goodness both from the heart's point of view and then from reason's point of view, and see where both meet.

The heart maintains that ethics is based on love. Let us explore this word. "Love" means harmony of being, community of being. Originally it applied to groups or persons who in some way belonged to one another, who had an inner reciprocal relationship, such as children and parents, married couples, or intimate friends. Morality requires that people we don't know should not be considered as strangers. That applies equally to those who are worse than strangers to us, because we feel an aversion toward them or because they have shown hostility to us. Even such people we must treat as our friends. In the last analysis the commandment of love means this: no one is a stranger to you; every man's welfare is your concern. We so often take for granted that some people are our immediate concern while others are a matter of indifference to us. Clearly this natural feeling is not permitted by ethical standards. Jesus rules out behaving toward one another as strangers when he says, "The other man must mean as much to you as your own self. You must feel his welfare as your own direct concern."

Further, let the heart explain the first commandment: "Thou shalt love thy God with all thy heart and with all thy mind and with all thy strength." To love God—this remote, unfathomable being! Here it is plain that the word "love," used ethically, is meant in a figurative sense. Should God, who has no need of us, be loved as though he were a creature we meet in daily life? In a human context, love means, for example, sharing an experience, showing compassion, and helping one another. But our love of God is akin to reverent love. God is infinite life. Thus the most elementary ethical principle, when understood by the heart, means that out of reverence for the unfathomable, infinite, and living Reality we call God, we must never consider ourselves strangers toward any human being. Rather, we must bind ourselves to the task of sharing his experiences and try being of help to him.

That, then, is what the heart says when it tries to give

meaning to the command of love toward God and neighbor.

But now let reason speak. Let us pretend that we have learned nothing about ethics from the past, and see how far we can get by pondering the forces that influence our actions. Can reason, too, make us step outside ourselves?

People often say that only egotism can be justified by reason. What can I do to have it easy? That is their reason's wisdom, nothing else. At most it can teach us a certain integrity and justice, and these things are more or less the recognized key to happiness. Reason is the desire for knowledge and the desire for happiness, and both are mysteriously connected with one another, in an inward way.

Desire for wisdom! Explore everything around you, penetrate to the furthest limits of human knowledge, and always you will come up against something inexplicable in the end. It is called life. It is a mystery so inexplicable that the knowledge of the educated and the ignorant is purely relative when contemplating it.

But what is the difference between the scientist who observes in his microscope the most minute and unexpected signs of life; and the old farmer who by contrast can barely read or write, who stands in springtime in his garden and contemplates the buds opening on the branches of his trees? Both are confronted with the riddle of life. One may be able to describe life in greater detail, but for both it remains equally inscrutable. All knowledge is, in the final analysis, the knowledge of life. All realization is amazement at this riddle of life—a reverence for life in its infinite and yet ever-fresh manifestations. How amazing this coming into being, living, and dying! How fantastic that in other existences something comes into being, passes away again, comes into being once more, and so forth from eternity to eternity! How can it be? We can do all things, and we can do nothing. For in all our wisdom we cannot create life. What we create is dead.

Life means strength, will, arising from the abyss, dissolving into the abyss again. Life is feeling, experience, suffering. If you study life deeply, looking with perceptive eyes into the vast animated chaos of this creation, its profundity will seize you suddenly wth dizziness. In everything you recognize yourself. The tiny beetle that lies dead in your path—it was a living creature, struggling for existence like yourself, rejoicing in the sun like you, knowing fear and pain like you. And now it is no more than decaying matter—which is what you will be sooner or later, too.

You walk outside and it is snowing. You carelessly shake the snow from your sleeves. It attracts your attention: a lacy snowflake glistens in your hand. You can't help looking at it. See how it sparkles in a wonderfully intricate pattern. Then it quivers, and the delicate needles of which it consists contract. It melts and lies dead in your hand. It is no more. The snowflake which fluttered down from infinite space upon your hand, where it sparkled and quivered and died—that is yourself. Wherever you see life—that is yourself!

What is this recognition, this knowledge within the reach of the most scientific and the most childlike? It is reverence for life, reverence for the unfathomable mystery we confront in our universe, an existence different in its outward appearance and yet inwardly of the same character as our own, terribly similar, awesomely related. The strangeness between us and other creatures is here removed.

Reverence for the infinity of life means removal of the alienation, restoration of empathy, compassion, sympathy. And so the final result of knowledge is the same as that required of us by the commandment of love. Heart and reason agree together when we desire and dare to be men who seek to fathom the depths of the universe.

Reason discovers the bridge between love for God and love for men—love for all creatures, reverence for all being, compassion with all life, however dissimilar to our own.

I cannot but have reverence for all that is called life. I cannot avoid compassion for everything that is called life. That is the beginning and foundation of morality. Once a man has experienced it and continues to do so— and he who has once experienced it will continue to do so —he is ethical. He carries his morality within him and can never lose it, for it continues to develop within him. He who has never experienced this has only a set of superficial principles. These theories have no root in him, they do not belong to him, and they fall off him. The worst is that the whole of our generation had only such a set of superficial principles. Then the time came to put the ethical code to the test, and it evaporated. For centuries the human race had been educated with only a set of superficial principles. We were brutal, ignorant, and heartless without being aware of it. We had no scale of values, for we had no reverence for life.

It is our duty to share and maintain life. Reverence concerning all life is the greatest commandment in its most elementary form. Or expressed in negative terms: "Thou shalt not kill." We take this prohibition so lightly, thoughtlessly plucking a flower, thoughtlessly stepping on a poor insect, thoughtlessly, in terrible blindness because everything takes its revenge, disregarding the suffering and lives of our fellow men, sacrificing them to trivial earthly goals.

Much talk is heard in our times about building a new

human race. How are we to build a new humanity? Only by leading men toward a true, inalienable ethic of our own, which is capable of further development. But this goal cannot be reached unless countless individuals will transform themselves from blind men into seeing ones and begin to spell out the great commandment which is: Reverence for Life. Existence depends more on reverence for life than the law and the prophets. Reverence for life comprises the whole ethic of love in its deepest and highest sense. It is the source of constant renewal for the individual and for mankind.

{ 16 }

*Ethics of Compassion**

For none of us liveth to himself, and no man dieth to himself.   ROMANS *14:7*

As I suggested last Sunday, we shall be discussing the problems of ethics in our next service.

When the scribe asked what was the greatest commandment in the Old Testament, Jesus replied by combining two precepts—love of God and love of neighbor. This, as we saw last week, raises the question of the nature of ethics, of the ultimate, fundamental principle of morality. We were not satisfied with the age-old answer that the essence of ethics is love. We went on to ask what love really is. What is the sort of love toward God which compels us to be kind to others? What does love for our neighbor mean? And we asked not only the heart but also the reason to explain the ethical. For, as we saw, the weakness of our times lies in a lack of a morality based on reason, a failure to discover an ethic immune to prejudice and passion. We never assume that reason and heart can walk effortlessly hand in

---

* *Preached Sunday, February 23, 1919, at the morning service at St. Nicolai's Church.*

hand. But the true heart is rational and the true reason has sensitivity. As we noticed, both heart and reason agree that in the last resort the good consists in elemental reverence of the enigma we call life, in reverence for all its manifestations, both great and small. The good is what preserves and advances life; evil is what hinders or destroys it. We are ethical if we abandon our stubbornness, if we surrender our strangeness toward other creatures and share in the life and the suffering that surround us. Only this quality makes us truly men. Only then do we possess an inalienable, continuously developing, and self-orienting ethic of our own.

"Reverence for life," "surrender of strangeness," "the urge to maintain life"—we hear these expressions around us, and they sound cold and shallow. But even if they are modest words they are rich in meaning. A seed is equally commonplace and insignificant, yet within it rests the germ of a lovely flower or a life-giving food. These simple words contain the basic attitude from which all ethical behavior develops, whether the individual is conscious of it or not. Thus the presupposition of morality is to share everything that goes on around us, not only in human life but in the life of all creatures. This awareness forces us to do all within our power for the preservation and advancement of life.

The great enemy of morality has always been indifference. As children, as far as our awareness of things went, we had an elementary capacity for compassion. But our capacity did not develop over the years in proportion to the growth of our understanding. This was uncomfortable and bewildering. We noticed so many people who no longer had compassion or empathy. Then we, too, suppressed our sensitivity so as to be like everyone else. We did not want to be different from them, and we did not know what to do. Thus many people become like houses in which one story after another has been vacated, a lifeless structure in which all windows look empty and strange, deserted.

To remain good means to remain wide awake. We are all like men walking in the bitter cold and snow. Woe to him who gives way to exhaustion, sits down, and falls asleep. He will never wake again. So our inmost moral being perishes when we are too tired to share the life and experiences and sufferings of the creatures around us. Woe to us if our sensitivity grows numb. It destroys our conscience in the broadest sense of the word: the consciousness of how we should act dies.

Reverence for life and sympathy with other lives is of supreme importance for this world of ours. Nature knows no similar reverence for life. It produces life a thousandfold in the most meaningful way and destroys it a thousandfold in the most meaningless way. In every stage of life, right up to the level of man, terrible ignorance lies over all creatures. They have the will to live but no capacity for compassion toward other creatures. They can't feel what happens inside others. They suffer but have no compassion. The great struggle for survival by which nature is maintained is in strange contradiction with itself. Creatures live at the expense of other creatures. Nature permits the most horrible cruelties to be committed. It impels insects by their instincts to bore holes into other insects, to lay their eggs in them so that maggots may grow there and live off the caterpillar, thus causing it a slow and painful death. Nature lets ants band together to attack poor little creatures and hound them to death. Look at the spider. How gruesome is the craft that nature taught it!

Nature looks beautiful and marvelous when you view it from the outside. But when you read its pages like a book, it is horrible. And its cruelty is so senseless! The most precious form of life is sacrificed to the lowliest. A child breathes the germs of tuberculosis. He grows and flourishes but is destined to suffering and a premature death because these lowly creatures multiply in his vital organs. How often in Africa have I been overcome with horror when I examined the blood of a patient who was suffering from sleeping sickness. Why did this man, his face contorted in pain, have to sit in front of me, groaning, "Oh, my head, my head"? Why should he have to suffer night after night and die a wretched death? Because there, under the microscope, were minute, pale corpuscles, one ten-thousandth of a millimeter long—not very many, sometimes such a very few that one had to look for hours to find them at all.

This, then, is the enigmatic contradiction in the will to live—life against life, causing suffering and death, innocent and yet guilty. Nature teaches cruel egotism, only briefly interrupted by the urge it has planted in creatures to offer love and assistance for their offspring as long as necessary.

Animals love their young so much that they are willing to die for them. They have this capacity for sympathy. Yet the self-perpetuation of the species makes all the more terrible their utter lack of concern for those beings unrelated to them.

The world given over to ignorance and egotism is like a valley shrouded in darkness. Only up on the peaks is there light. All must live in the darkness. Only one creature can escape and catch a glimpse of the light: the highest creature, man. He is permitted to achieve the knowledge of reverence for life. His is the privilege of achieving the knowledge of shared experience and compassion, of transcending the ignorance in which the rest of creation pines.

And this understanding is the great event in the evolution of life. Through it truth and goodness appear in the world. Light shines above the darkness. The highest form of life has been attained, life sharing the life of others, in which one existence feels the pulse of the whole world and life becoming aware of its all-embracing existence. Individual isolation ceases. Outside life streams like a flood into our own.

We live in the world, and the world lives in us. Even this knowledge raises a host of questions. Why do the laws of nature and the laws of ethics diverge so sharply? Why cannot human reason simply take over and develop its discoveries into an expression of life in nature? Why must rationality come into such terrible conflict with everything it sees? Why must it discover that the law of its own being is so utterly different from the laws governing the world? Why must it be at odds with the world just when it discovers the principle of the good? Why must we experience this conflict without the hope of ever finding solution? Why, instead of harmony, is there cleavage? And further, God is the power that sustains the universe. Why is this God who reveals himself in nature the denial of everything we feel to be ethical? How can a force rationally create life and irrationally destroy it at the same time? How can we reconcile God as a force of nature with God as ethical will, the God of love as we must conceive him when we have risen to a higher ideal of life, to reverence for life, to empathy and compassion?

Several Sundays ago, when we were trying to clarify optimistic and pessimistic views of life, I told you that it is a great misfortune for mankind that we cannot offer a harmonious philosophy of life. The more knowledge increases, the more it deprives us of such a possibility. Not only because it becomes increasingly plain how little we can grasp in knowledge, but also because the contradictions in life become increasingly evident. We know in part, as St. Paul says. But this is not putting it strongly enough. The greater obstacle is that our knowledge affords only a glimpse into insoluble contradictions, all of which can be traced back to the one basic contradiction: the law according to which all this illogic occurs has, in itself, nothing that we recognize and feel to be ethical.

Instead of being able to anchor our morality in a coherent world-view and a harmonious concept of God, we must constantly defend it against the contradictions arising from our world view, contradictions that threaten it like a destructive breaker. We must erect a dam—but will it hold?

The other threat to our capacity and our will to empathy is nagging doubt. What is the use of it? you think. Your most strenuous efforts to prevent suffering, to ease suffering, to preserve life, are nothing compared to the anguish remaining in the world around you, the wounds you are powerless to heal. Certainly, it is dreadful to be reminded of the extent of our helplessness. It is worse still to realize how much suffering we ourselves cause others without being able to prevent it.

You are walking along a path in the woods. The sunshine makes lovely patterns through the trees. The birds are singing, and thousands of insects buzz happily in the air. But as you walk along the path, you are involuntarily the cause of death. Here you trod on an ant and tortured it; there you squashed a beetle; and over there your unknowing step left a worm writhing in agony. Into the glorious melody of life you weave a discordant strain of suffering and death. You are guilty, though it is no fault of your own. And, despite all your good intentions, you are conscious of a terrible inability to help as you would like to. Then comes the voice of the tempter: Why torture

yourself? It is no good. Give up, stop caring. Be uncon-
cerned and unfeeling like everybody else.

Still another temptation arises—compassion really involves you in suffering. Anyone who experiences the woes
of this world within his heart can never again feel the sur-
face happiness that human nature desires. When hours of
contentment and joy come, the compassionate man cannot
give himself unreservedly to them, for he can never forget
the suffering he has experienced with others. What he has
seen stays with him. The anguished faces of the poor
return; the cries of the sick echo in his mind; he remembers
the man whose hard lot he once read about—and darkness
shuts out the light of his joy. Darkness returns again and
again. In cheerful company he suddenly becomes absent-
minded. And the tempter says again: You can't live like
this. You must be able to detach yourself from what is
depressing around you. Don't be so sensitive. Teach yourself the necessary indifference, put on an armor, be thoughtless like everybody else if you want to live a sensible life.
In the end we are ashamed to know of the great experience
of empathy and compassion. We keep it secret from one
another and pretend it is foolish, a weakness we outgrow
when we begin to be "reasonable" people.

These three great temptations unobtrusively wreck the
presupposition of all goodness. Guard against them.
Counter the first temptation by saying that for you to
share experience and to lend a helping hand is an ab-
solute inward necessity. Your utmost attempts will be but
a drop in the ocean compared with what needs to be done,
but only this attitude will give meaning and value to your
life. Wherever you are, as far as you can, you should bring
redemption, redemption from the misery brought into the
world by the self-contradictory will of life, redemption that
only he who has this knowledge can bring. The small

amount you are able to do is actually much if it only relieves pain, suffering, and fear from any living being, be it human or any other creature. The preservation of life is the true joy.

As for the other temptation, the fear that compassion will involve you in suffering, counter it with the realization that the sharing of sorrow expands your capacity to share joy as well. When you callously ignore the suffering of others, you lose the capacity to share their happiness, too. And however little joy we may see in this world, the sharing of it, together with the good we ourselves create, produces the only happiness which makes life tolerable. And finally, you have no right to say: I will be this, or I will be that, because I think one way will make me happier than another. No, you must be what you ought to be, a true, knowing man, a man who identifies himself with the world, a man who experiences the world within himself. Whether you are happier by the ordinary standards of happiness or not doesn't matter. The secret hour does not require of us that we should be happy—to obey the call is the only thing that satisfies deeply.

So I tell you, don't let your hearts grow numb. Stay alert. It is your soul which matters. If only these words—words in which I am laying bare my inmost thoughts—could force you who are with me here to destroy the deceit with which the world tries to put us to sleep! If only you would all stop being thoughtless and stop flinching from the challenge to learn reverence for life and true empathy, if only you could be absorbed in compassionate awareness, I would rest content. I would consider my work blessed, even if I knew I would not be allowed to preach tomorrow or that my preaching thus far had been useless or that I would never again be able to achieve anything else.

I who generally shrink from influencing others, because

of the responsibility it entails, now wish I had the power to transform you, and make you have compassion, until each one of you had experienced the great suffering from which there is no escape and had gained the wisdom that compassion brings. Then I could tell myself that you are on the way to real goodness and that you will never lose it again. None of us lives for himself. May this word pursue us. May it never let us rest until we are laid into our graves.

{ 17 }

*Fulfill Your Destiny**

I

In everything give thanks: for this is the will of God in Christ Jesus concerning you.

1 THESSALONIANS 5:*18*

"INGRATITUDE IS THE THANKS you expect from the world," a saying goes. It expresses an angry truth experienced by everyone at one time or another. These words contain more than the simple observation that the world tends to repay favors with indifference. An echo is heard of the sentiment: "There is no sense in doing good." That is the tragedy. The prevalence of ingratitude leaves much unsatisfaction in the human heart. Ingratitude fails to produce much good that might otherwise be done. Ingratitude stifles the spirit that is eager for ethical action in the world.

Of course, when people so readily agree with the pessimism of the proverb, they are not always being honest. Have we who complain of ingratitude looked only for the

---

* *Part I preached Sunday, July 27, 1919; Part II preached Sunday, August 17, 1919; at the morning services at St. Nicolai's Church.*

gratitude we think we have a right to expect as men of moral behavior? Let us be truthful with ourselves. Often when we have been disappointed by receiving no thanks, we should not have expected any at all, at any rate not in the superficial forms. All of us are strongly tempted to use the good we do as a trap to ensnare another. "How can you forget what I have done for you?" is the reproach we use to taunt someone in a time when he does not agree with us or refuses a request of ours. So we drag him along in our lasso of gratitude until he cannot bear it any longer. If he reacts in self-defense, we call on our neighbors to witness his ingratitude. We puff up in righteous indignation. Our associates agree with us and aid in humiliating the ingrate. But what was the truth of the matter? It is *we* who are guilty of ingratitude far more than the other fellow. For we misused gratitude to blackmail him. All of us have succumbed to this temptation, because ugliness appears in such an honorable disguise and acts so virtuously that we fail to recognize it for what it is. Without thinking what we are doing, we may even go so far as to expect the person in our debt to act against his own conviction and conscience. So beware. If you are chagrined at the ingratitude of others, step aside for a moment and quietly ask yourself whether you are really justified in expecting thanksgiving in the light of morality and conscience. Think how you yourself have suffered when men expected gratitude from you and humiliated you.

Other demands of gratitude, asked by the thoughtless person, must be refused by the ethical person. I mean the silly and superficial expectations we attach as strings to the good we do. When we have done people a good turn, we expect them to speak well of us. If they don't do it loudly enough, we think they are being ungrateful. When you feel the words "Ingratitude is the thanks you get from the

world" forming on the tip of your tongue—stop and listen. Perhaps it is the voice of vanity in your heart. If you can still be honest with yourself, you will often find this to be so. Then tell your heart to be quiet, and revise your notions of what gratitude is entitled to expect. Take warning from the realization that thoughtless people generally complain most about ingratitude. Those who think seriously about the ingratitude they encounter do not find it as easy to be indignant.

But granted that we have so trained ourselves that the ugly, vain, and superficial have no part in our expectations of gratitude; granted, too, that we have been so successful in purifying our motives that we really try to do good for its own sake and not in the hope of being appreciated—we shall still be hurt by the prevalence of ingratitude. What men can and ought to give one another by way of mutual thankfulness is more than mere satisfaction derived from expectations that are more or less justified and pure. Such gratitude as we do meet helps us to believe in this world's goodness, and it thus encourages us to do good. The desire to protect ourselves against ingratitude is of no help at all. Disappointment that wounds our soul is a demoralizing thing. Good seed sown in good earth sprouts in all weathers, yet its growth is more flourishing in favorable weather than in unfavorable. All of us find it difficult to hold fast to an optimistic philosophy of life that gives us strength to do good. That is why ingratitude, which is constantly killing our enthusiasm, is one of evil's worst forces.

None of us is immune from this evil. We refuse one another the services we could render. It is not just that we refuse to show gratitude because it requires some effort on our part. Even the kind of gratitude expressible in thoughts, words, or small acts of kindness requiring little effort on our part is lacking. Without great exertion, with only a little attentiveness, we could give each other much cause for contentment. But we fail to do so. That is just the problem.

When are we habitually ungrateful?

If anyone were to tell you that you are ungrateful like everyone else, you would be shocked at the very suggestion. Of course we can all remember occasions when we did act ungratefully. Such memories are burned into our souls even when we deny them to the world. We are inclined to justify our lapses as passing weaknesses which do not condemn us to classification among the ungrateful. We can glibly take this attitude because we are convinced that we have no reason to reproach ourselves for ungrateful acts.

Let us face up to it and examine ourselves now. On the whole, we don't believe we are among the ungrateful. Could we be deluding ourselves? The current spirit of ingratitude reveals itself not only in the commission of ungrateful acts but also in the omission of expressions of appreciation. Perhaps I can more or less absolve myself from ungrateful actions, or at least I think I can, but can I equally claim to have shown gratitude whenever I have had cause to do so? As soon as we spotlight the word "ingratitude" from both sides, our confidence begins to shake. We all do wrong, daily, by soaking up good deeds and acts of kindness as sandy soil soaks up water. The desire to show ourselves grateful is not ordinarily the motivating power of our lives. We have not yet taken to heart what the apostle meant in that great saying: "In every thing give thanks." By the standards of morality we are all guilty of ingratitude, even if we do not have that reputation among our acquaintances.

In order to clarify the general question: Are you grate-

ful? we have to divide it into two parts. First: Do you *feel* sufficient gratitude? Second: Do you *show* sufficient gratitude?

Let us take the first question. Do you feel sufficient gratitude? To appreciate it properly we must remind ourselves how often we have not been aware of gratitude at the moment when the good deed was being done for us. Rather, it dawned upon us gradually, until afterward we were surprised at ourselves for not instantly recognizing the value of the kindly act as it was being done. None of us can look back on his youth without embarrassment, for we accepted so much without any feeling of appreciation. Sadly we contemplate the graves of teachers who worked so hard to educate us or of others who helped us along in selfless ways. They passed on without our having shown them what they meant to us. We could not show it because we could not evaluate it, and we could not evaluate it because we never gave it a minute's thought. As we grew older we learned by experience to appreciate these things more. But as for our imperfect sensitivity concerning acts of kindness received—every one of us remains incredibly immature despite our graying hair! We walk along in a dreamland, accepting what others do for us as the natural thing, when in fact it is not natural at all. And yet we expect that others will show their appreciation and be deeply moved by the least thing we do for them.

We all make the mistake of relying on our natural sense of gratitude, thinking that this is sufficient to make us grateful people. Compared with true gratitude, this feeling is what grass is to wheat. Grass develops ears, too, which blossom and bear grain like wheat. But these meager grains cannot sustain our life like those from the improved strains that have been developed from grasses. So, too, we must perfect and ennoble through self-training those natural instincts of gratitude that are a dogma of our life. If we fail to do so, what usually happens is this: our innate self-esteem will encourage us in the illusion that we are genuinely grateful people.

Developing a true sense of gratitude involves taking absolutely nothing for granted, wherever it be, whatever its source. Rather, we always look for the friendly intention behind the deed and learn to appreciate it. Make a point of measuring at its true value every act of kindness you receive from other men. Nothing that may happen to you is purely accidental. Everything can be traced back to a will for good directed in your favor. If you try seriously and continuously to train yourself in gratitude, you will have trouble with the obstinate man within you. When he expects appreciation he bucks like a stubborn horse before a ditch. He always knows a way around in order to devaluate what he has received and indicate he wants more. There is no end to his tricks. The commonest excuse we use to avoid this sense of gratitude is: "The other fellow was only doing his duty." Thus our sense of gratitude toward our closest friends is devalued and we reach the sad point of accepting acts of kindness from those dearest to us without giving them the word of encouragement they need. Isn't this lack of gratitude toward our closest friends responsible for the estrangement and misunderstanding that can grow up between us? So when you judge what others have done for you, don't say that the other fellow was simply doing his duty. The only point you must take into consideration is his kind intention toward you and his goodness in putting it into effect. The intention that represents the reality is our concern.

Beware also of the double trick the ungrateful man within you likes to play. If the service rendered to you is a minor one, he rationalizes: "Well, it was not that much bother for the other fellow." If he knows that the service was a great deal of trouble, he minimizes it: "Well, I didn't benefit that much from what he did." Out of inner fear that we might owe something to another, we behave as though we were haggling over a deal. Never assent to such behavior; always put the highest value on acts of kindness. Every time somebody does something for you, look at it from his standpoint as well as from your own.

Suppose someone has done you a great service with little effort on his part. Perhaps he has helped you to get a job by going somewhere to recommend you. Or he may have happened by chance to be in a position to help you without any great exertion on his part. Perhaps even he himself has no idea just how much he has done for you. You, however, must consider just how much it meant to you for him to do this service at that particular time, and you should feel toward him forever the gratitude he deserves. If the service is of little value to you, remember that you cannot possibly know how hard or how easy it may have been for him. Things that are insignificant outwardly sometimes represent a great deal of trouble or the overcoming of serious obstacles. You ask for information and receive a letter which provides it. The letter may represent ten minutes' work. But the man who wrote it may be accosted from many sides because he is obliging and has many such letters to write or many such errands to perform. You are indebted to him not only because of the letter he wrote to you or the errand he did, but for his willingness to surrender to those in need the time another man would have used for personal recreation. The letter of information he wrote to you may have been written at midnight or on a Sunday afternoon. It always seems to me that those people who themselves are not obliging are seemingly least appreciative of the little services done for them. They do not know from their own experience the work or the sacrifice involved in even a small act of kindness.

As you train yourself in gratitude, do not forget, in addition to obvious acts of kindness, those thoughtful deeds which are inconspicuous or whose recollection might prove an embarrassment. Maybe someone has had a hold over you because he heard you make a careless remark, or he knows of something you forgot to do, or he is party to one of your secrets. Such a person can make things awkward for you, perhaps even disgrace you. But your friend has not done so. Now, perhaps, this is all in the past. But do not forget what you owe him, even if you find it humiliating.

In self-training in the feeling of gratitude you are entirely on your own. Your nearest and dearest will never teach you to show gratitude. They will always confirm you in your delusion that you are indeed an appreciative person. If they laugh at you for making such a to-do about what someone may have done for you, or if you are no longer able to confide your genuine feeling because they do not understand the depth of your feeling, then you are on the right track. Why is it that a string plucked on a violin or a harp has such a lovely tone, but a string plucked on a table can hardly be heard? The sensitive soundbox vibrates along with it. Thus, the good deed you meet in this world will have a true and lovely tone only if it resounds—prepared for by a grateful mind.

Do you show sufficient gratitude? This second question guides you along the road of self-training no less than the first about feeling the gratitude. The world is such a cold place because we do not show enough gratitude to those to whom we do feel grateful. Thus they conclude that we are ungrateful, and it hurts them.

Why do we so often miss the chance to express the gratitude we feel? It is due to thoughtlessness and laziness.

We do not pay enough attention to it. When Jesus healed the ten lepers, only one came back to say thank you. Were the other nine ungrateful? Not at all. Perhaps they thought of him just as warmly as the grateful leper and spoke of him with emotion. But when they had shown themselves to the priest in Jerusalem and were allowed to go home, only one of them thought of returning first to the Lord. The others went back to their villages. They forgot to express thanks because they were already absorbed in their next move. We do just that, hundreds and hundreds of times, in things both small and great. Recently a nurse who looks after surgery patients told me, "Half of the patients in my ward go home without even saying goodbye to me." Are all of these ungrateful? Surely not. Rather, when the day of their discharge comes, they are so preoccupied with their departure, and pay so much attention to the relatives who come to fetch them, that they forget to thank the nurse, unless she happens to be around. They are in too much of a hurry to take the time to go and look for her and shake her hand. In the heat of the moment they fail because they have never trained themselves to say thank you.

During the war many prisoners or wounded received favors from friends, and perhaps also from enemies. When they parted, there were many assurances: I will never forget you; I will write to you at the first opportunity, I will keep in touch with you. Of a thousand letters so intended barely a dozen ever got written. Then the distant friends complain bitterly that gratitude does not exist. In fact it is there, present in the heart. But it may as well not exist because the people concerned don't make the effort to write such a letter, though they do find the time to read three or four newspapers every day from beginning to end.

Never put off gratitude. The Bible says, "Let not the sun go down upon your wrath." Let this be true of gratitude, too. Express it the same day you feel it. A friend from the country may send you some fruit. You are touched by the gift and determine to write to him soon. A week later, your letter still unwritten, he comes to town and asks in the course of conversation whether the fruit has arrived. What was heartfelt thanks now becomes embarrassed apologies on both sides.

If we think seriously only for just five minutes where we have failed in showing expressions of gratitude, the painful memories which come to mind must make us squirm. How can we count the words and letters of thanks left unsaid and unwritten, the personal calls over which we procrastinated!

We leave much undone because we forget. We intend to do other things but put them off and never get around to doing them. Finally the occasion for our thanks seems so long age that we can scarcely come back to it with good grace. Sometimes, too, someone may have died before we could get around to expressing the gratitude we intended. Added to the pain of losing him is another sorrow—our ingratitude, which we can now no longer remedy.

In other cases we may have expressed our thanks, but years later we fail to reiterate that we still remember his kindness, even when opportunity to do so arises. It is quite incredible how shyness, stupidity, carelessness, and laziness combine to make us into ungrateful people. How feebly we guard against these temptations, how defenseless we are against them! That is why we must train ourselves never to postpone the word or the visit to show our gratitude.

Gratitude is never fully completed. No, you must show your benefactor later on, whenever the opportunity arises, that your gratitude is still alive in your heart. Just as there

must be no procrastination or postponement of your gratitude, so it must never cease even if subsequent circumstances occur. A man has done a good deed for you. Later
on, something comes up between you, through no fault of
your own. He disagrees with your views or disapproves of
your relationship with this or that person. He may even
have done you harm or alienated you by some action. To
be at odds with those we have cared about is hard. It is
still harder when it happens with someone we were bound
to by ties of gratitude. Anyone who has been through this
experience in life knows the complications that arise in
such a case. But whatever may happen, never say to yourself: "I'm through with him." Let the memory of your
gratitude survive every subsequent event. And should an
opportunity arise for you to let him know that thankfulness is still alive in your heart despite what has happened since, don't miss the chance of telling him about it.
Don't let shyness stop you; don't be worried he might
take it amiss or laugh at you. Consider the essential meaning of gratitude: a human being is eternally joined to you
by mysterious bonds created through a deed done. He has
a claim on you, a claim not based on general laws which
he expects but one given by you recognized and acknowledged by yourself. You must undertake to give him whatever this claim demands, wherever and whenever you can.
Never regard the person to whom you owe a debt of
gratitude as just any man. He is someone special, someone you regard as sacred.

II

The showing of gratitude by word of mouth and acts
of kindness is expected of us in daily routine. Only in a
small fraction of cases are we able to prove our indebted-

ness by acts demanding considerable effort on our part. To train ourselves to do these acts means to take up the battle against our lack of character and our love of comfort. How blithely and how skillfully we avoid acts of thankfulness! The best among us are good at deceiving ourselves, a fact which should make us shudder when we dare admit it to ourselves. To count up the disappointments we have inflicted on those who needed us and had a claim on our gratitude is shattering for every one of us. Who does not see indelibly printed on his mind the eyes of those who have looked at him reproachfully? Often the sacrifices asked of us were not even large. They were services we could easily have rendered if only we had been so inclined.

Don't be like so many who care only about getting rid of these memories, who in fact detest the ones they left in the lurch because those people haunt them with humiliating memories. Experience this humiliation as something that makes you serious and strong for what you will have to give in the future. Only he who can look back on his life and feel grief and fear of ingratitude is capable of gratitude.

If you are to put gratitude into action, it is important that you not wait until it is demanded of you. Whenever you sense that someone may need help, don't wait to be asked, but offer it immediately. Remember the times you had to approach someone to remind him of his debt to you and then beg him to do some service for you. How difficult such requests are! Why don't we spare each other when we are able to? Be sensitive and skillful in rendering gratitude. So often we humiliate and hurt a person who is obligated to us in such a case.

Take care you don't let your gratitude be stifled because of fear of men. Many services we render as proof of our gratitude consist in recommending people, perhaps vouching for them or taking their side when they are being slandered or to protect them in case of injustice. Shyness and lack of character overpower you and provide excuses for avoiding these duties. They tell you that you might be able and would be happy to serve in every other way. But to distinguish yourself in *this* way is not your business; you would be doing them little good, in fact nothing, compared with the misunderstandings and unpleasantnesses you might make yourself vulnerable to. These are just the sort of arguments that slippery lawyers will use. If you don't choke resistance off while you are under the influence of the first good impulse, you will succumb. And once you have submitted to fear of men, they will have you forever in their power.

Another thing to remember about the repayment of gratitude is: Don't start calculating whether or not the service you are performing is greater than the one you received. Fate might demand that you repay something small by a larger one, maybe even with something really great. Don't argue with fate. That same fate orders others to repay you in the same way, with great benefits in return for small ones. Its ways are strange and defy examination. Comply with them, in giving as in receiving.

The proof of gratitude is greater and broader in scope than simply helping people who have done us some service, should the opportunity arise. It consists in doing good simply because I have received benefits. Often we are unable to repay a person for a kindness received. He may never be in a position to need our services, or maybe he is no longer in this world. Anyway, it is impossible always to thank particular individuals for all the kindnesses you have received. Often you don't even know the source.

A man is brought into the Strasbourg hospital for surgery. Whom does he thank if he is restored to health? Not only the surgeon who operated on him, the assistants who bandaged him, and the nurses who took care of him. Others, too, who exist in the background of the past. The hospital stands there to take him in because of those philanthropists who founded it by their donations. He can be gently lulled to sleep so that his operation does not mean ghastly pain (which would have been the case a hundred years ago) because of those scientists who discovered ether and chloroform and those volunteers who acted as guinea pigs to test such drugs. It at last has become possible to perform surgery antiseptically, without fear of infection (which used to be the great danger in all surgery), because of the gift of the Viennese physician Semmelweis. He observed that all infections were caused by invisible dirt brought into the wound by the surgeon's hands and found infection could be prevented if the surgeon first washed his hands with a disinfectant, chloride of lime, the first antiseptic he turned to. These unknown benefits from the past are of help in every operation, and the patient owes his recovery to many people toward whom he will never have a chance to express gratitude. So instead, in the name of his inaccessible benefactors, he must repay it to those who need him.

So let the good you do in gratitude match the benefits you have received. Balance the books inside of you, and see if you are repaying in full the amount you owe to unknown men and to fate itself. Have you been helped when you were ill? Then know that you have to do something for someone sick. Has someone offered you a loan in time of need? If you know someone in similar straits, assist him in gratitude for the help you have received. Have you turned up somewhere as a stranger and been given hospitality? Now *you* must do the same for a stranger. Has someone gone on an errand for you or stood up for you? In return, serve someone else in like manner. Has a person helped you by giving you the right teaching to achieve something worthwhile? Look around and see if there isn't someone in equal need of you. Have you been given without charge something for which you usually have to pay? Give someone something for which you would normally expect payment. Has someone taken time for you which he could hardly afford to give? This obligates you to take time for another, even if you are overworked. This is what you must do all your life, in things both great and small. Don't talk about it. It is an item in a ledger only you can or should see, and it is nobody else's business. Only be sure that the balance is correct.

Certain plants in nature spread below the earth. The root grows in the soil and sends up shoots at intervals so that eventually several plants are standing near one another, apparently independent and unconnected. Yet in reality they all came from a common root that existed at the start. That is how deeds of kindness should spread. Let the kindness you receive send out fertile roots from which new plants may grow. You must learn to understand the secret of gratitude, for it is more than what we call a virtue. Learn to see it as a mysterious law of existence. In obedience to it we have to fulfill our destiny.

This involves a mystical view of life. True. But whenever we penetrate to the heart of things, we always find a mystery. Life and all that goes with it is unfathomable. What appears to belong to the realm of everyday life assumes an unexpectedly deep and consequential character as soon as we analyze it to the limit. Knowledge of life is the recognition of the mysterious. To act justly means to obey the laws that arise from this recognition of the mysterious.

If you are striving to fulfill the noble law of gratitude, the effort will bring you a peculiar bonus. The ingratitude you encounter will cause you less suffering than you experienced before. Watch yourself from day to day, and see how often you are remiss in showing gratitude. You will then not judge others as harshly as people do when they have not undertaken such self-analysis. The feeling of guilt which burdens you will make you indulgent toward others, for you realize how hard it is to show gratitude to everyone for everything. The failure of others to give you your due won't hurt you as much as it did when you were naïvely indignant.

But further, you know that there is more appreciation around than meets the eye. Much heartfelt gratitude never reaches the point of being expressed in word or deed. This thought will be a consolation to you when others are beside themselves. The ingratitude of this world as a power of evil has lost much of its former strength over you. As for all those thoughtless and ungrateful people, you can leave them the proverb: "Ingratitude is the thanks you get from the world." But you—you can smile at it. You have looked into the heart of things and seen behind them, and there is no need for you to stop at such a gloomy piece of wisdom.

Editor's Postscript:
Albert Schweitzer as Preacher

THE LIFE AND WORK of Albert Schweitzer have been examined in countless publications and from many different angles. The autobiographical writings and reports of Schweitzer himself from Lambaréné, place a considerable amount of material at our disposal. But one aspect of his life, a very important one for him, has remained almost entirely unknown: his activity as a preacher. Only a few people are alive today who sat under the pulpit of the young curate more than fifty years ago and now retain some impression of his preaching.

His activity as a preacher extended from 1898 until 1913. After an interruption, it was resumed once more in 1918 and continued until 1921. Two draft sermons also survive from 1934, both on the theme of forgiveness. They show that Schweitzer—apart from his daily devotions and services at Lambaréné—sometimes preached while he was staying in Europe.

During 1898 Albert Schweitzer substituted from time to time for his father at Günsbach, a village in Upper Alsace. On December 1, 1899, he became assistant minister at the Church of St. Nicolai in Strasbourg, and he was ordained on January 29, 1900. On February 25, which happened to be the Sunday before Lent, he preached his trial sermon on the text "Rejoice always" (1 Thess. 5:16). After July 15, when he completed his second examination, he became a full-fledged associate minister there.

Albert Schweitzer was generally responsible for the afternoon services, but later he gradually assumed responsibility for the morning services too. He said of sermon preparation: "I used to write my sermons out in full, often making two or three drafts before begining the fair copy. When delivering the sermons, however, I did not tie myself to this outline, which I had carefully learnt by heart, but often gave the discourse a quite different form."*

Albert Schweitzer relinquished his curacy in the spring of 1912. On March 9, 1913, he delivered a farewell sermon before leaving for Lambaréné. After his release from a French internment camp at the end of World War I, he again accepted the office of preacher at St. Nicolai's until April 1921, but with long interruptions during his travels abroad.

It would be wrong to conclude, simply because we happen to know so little about Albert Schweitzer's preaching, that he regarded it as a sideline. On the contrary, preaching was for him a heartfelt necessity, and giving it up after his departure for Lambaréné meant a great sacrifice for him. We find definite proof of this in his own reminiscenses of the year 1899:

"Theobald Ziegler urged me to qualify as a *Privatdozent* in the Faculty of Philosophy, but I decided for the theological. Ziegler hinted to me that if I were a *Privatdozent* in philosophy people would not be pleased to see me active as a preacher as well. But to me preaching was a necessity of my being. I felt it as something wonderful that I was

---

* *Out of My Life and Thought* (New York: Henry Holt Company, 1933), p. 39.

allowed to address a congregation every Sunday about the deepest questions of life.*

"The text of my last sermon to the congregation of St. Nicolai's was St. Paul's words of blessing in his Epistle to the Philippians: 'The peace of God which passeth all understanding, keep your hearts and minds in Christ Jesus,' a text with which all through the years I had closed every service I had held.

"Not to preach any more, not to lecture any more, was for me a great sacrifice, and till I left for Africa I avoided, as far as possible, going past either St. Nicolai's or the University, because the very sight of the places where I had carried on work which I should never resume was too painful to me."†

Albert Schweitzer the preacher is overshadowed by the thinker, the physician, and the musician. The reason for this is that his sermons never reached the public. Actually he did periodically consider publishing them under the title "Meditations from St. Nicolai's." But nothing ever came of this plan, and later he gave it up. There were serious reasons for his reluctance. The tremendous load of work on his shoulders, especially while he was studying medicine, meant that only rarely could he work through his sermons to the extent that would have been necessary for publication. Many of his manuscripts are only rough drafts. Others are carefully developed to a point, but the ending consists of no more than a sketchy summary. Schweitzer had to utilize every spare moment. His manuscripts contain such notes as: "Rough draft produced in the waiting room in Paris en route to Le Havre, February 7, 5:00–8:00 A.M."

---

* *Ibid.*, p. 36.
† *Ibid.*, p. 134.

Publication would have required a careful revision of all the manuscripts and the elimination of all the provisional elements. For this there was insufficient time, and Schweitzer would not publish anything in fragmentary form.

Several excerpts were printed by Fritz Wartenweiler in his essay in the *Festschrift* honoring the Doctor of the Primeval Forest on his eightieth birthday.* Wartenweiler deserves the credit for having taken an interest in Schweitzer's sermons at quite an early date.

For the preservation of these sermons we are indebted to Mrs. Annie Stinnes Fischer, who took the trouble to copy carefully about 150 manuscripts during World War II. These typescripts survived the war, but the original handwritten manuscripts were burned in an air raid on Stuttgart. Except for the last sermon, the material in this book has been based on Mrs. Fischer's typescripts, which have been left unaltered as far as possible. Obvious errors in the copy, or grammatical slips which seemed to be obvious errors, have been corrected without note. Since the copy gives the impression of meticulous care, the alterations in the text are only of a very minor kind.

Originally there must have been many more manuscripts of Schweitzer's sermons. For certain years we possess twenty, for others only four, and for one year none at all. Some of the series are incomplete. Furthermore, we know of texts on which Schweitzer preached on particular occasions, but the sermons themselves are missing. It is possible that more sermons will come to light when Schweitzer's literary remains at Günsbach have been sorted through. However, we would not expect drastic changes in

---

* *Ehrfurcht vor dem Leben* (Paul Haupt), pp. 104–14.

the overall picture, at most only an enrichment of what we already have. The most important sermons are obviously preserved in our collection.

In 1965, we had some correspondence with Dr. Schweitzer about the possibility of publishing the sermons. This collection was about to be sent for final perusal and decision to Lambaréné when news reached us of the jungle doctor's illness, soon followed by his death.

The seventeen sermons published in this volume are only a small part of the material extant, and a still smaller part of the complete collection of Albert Schweitzer's sermons. Our principles of selection were as follows:

To begin with, we eliminated all of the sermons that existed in unfinished form. Unfortunately, this meant that we had to drop some that were of great elemental power and deep penetration, and some with great beauty of language. A series of sermons had to be excluded because their endings were only sketched in. Our selection from the completed sermons was made so as to give the most typical and all-round picture of the preacher at St. Nicolai's. For this reason we included also a sermon of the very young Schweitzer from a series he preached on the Beatitudes. This sermon, when compared with later ones, shows how he developed during the Strasbourg years. It is noticeable how Schweitzer progresses from more conventional thoughts to those specifically his own, and how his language gains in pregnancy and imagery. Further, we have included some sermons from a series dealing with ethical questions. These date from after his return from the French internment camp and display a style entirely different from the earlier ones. They are important mainly for the understanding of Albert Schweitzer himself, because, being now completely absorbed with the ideal of reverence for life, which he discovered in Africa, he speaks about it for the first time before a large congregation. It should be noted that these sermons were delivered prior to the publication of *Civilization and Ethics,* and it is significant that Schweitzer chose his parish in Strasbourg and his office as a preacher to reveal this, his inmost thought, for the first time. We can clearly sense the inner emotion that moved the preacher in these hours, so decisive for his own life, on February 16 and 23, 1919. These sermons supplement our understanding of Reverence for Life, especially in the way they illuminate the connection between this ethic and the New Testament commandment of love as Schweitzer saw it.

Apart from this, it seemed important to include sermons for the festivals of the Christian year. It is remarkable how many of the complete sermons are for Advent, Christmas, and Passiontide. The coming of Christ and, still more, the mystery of the Lord's suffering must have been Albert Schweitzer's great and recurrent concerns as a preacher. He was also interested in Pentecost and the subject of the Holy Spirit.

Apart from the great festivals of the church, we find a remarkable number of sermons dealing with the subject of missions. Obviously Schweitzer was deeply moved by this subject before going to Lambaréné. Sermons on this topic generally deal with the same theme—answering various objections to missionary work. From the many sermons on missions, we have chosen the one of January 6, 1905, because in it Schweitzer develops his thoughts on atonement, which was very important to him. In this sermon he gives us an insight into how he arrived at this conclusion. The sermon of November 20, 1904, is one of the many harvest and Thanksgiving sermons, indicating how important this occasion was for the preacher.

Schweitzer's style of preaching is highly individual. Basing our interpretation on the whole collection of sermon material, we may recognize the following points as typical:

1. Schweitzer mainly uses New Testament texts and only rarely a text from the Old Testament. Although this is the obvious approach for a New Testament scholar, yet his predilection is so plain that his education cannot be the sole explanation. Schweitzer himself was conscious of his inclination and spoke of it on one of the few occasions when he chose an Old Testament text. "I seldom preach to you about the prophets and sometimes I reproach myself for this. For there are such wonderful sayings in their books. It says in the Scriptures: 'But when that which is perfect is come, then that which is in part shall be done away.' Because we have that which is perfect in the sayings of the Lord we speak so rarely of the imperfect—the prophets."* Of the eight Schweitzer sermons now available on Old Testament texts, four are from the year 1902.

Within the New Testament, Schweitzer obviously preferred the Synoptics (Matthew, Mark, and Luke) and the writings of Paul. Half of the approximately 150 sermons, namely, 76, are based on Synoptic texts. Among these, Matthew has the main share, 46 sermons. There are 36 based on texts from St. Paul in addition to two sermons on the Epistle to the Ephesians.

His preference for the New Testament does not mean that Schweitzer disregarded the Old Testament, for in his Bible study in Lambaréné, which extended over several

---

* Sermon of October 7, 1902, on Zechariah 4:6.

decades, he periodically used the Old Testament. But his piety centered entirely on Jesus himself.

2. Schweitzer generally chose short texts, usually a saying full of meaning. He did not preach homilies in the sense so common nowadays, paraphrasing whole chapters verse by verse. Nor did he simply preach sermons on set topics, although they were used on occasions such as Thanksgiving, Ash Wednesday, Missionary Sunday, and so forth. Rather, his method was to be moved and led by the saying and to explore it. In particular he allowed himself to be led by the picture suggested by a word. A typical example of this is the sermon of December 10, 1904, on the subject of plowing.

3. Schweitzer never preached doctrinal or teaching sermons. Nor was he moralistic. Rather, he was concerned with the souls of his flock. The legend has arisen—and occurs in several books—that his preaching was "entirely moralistic." This verdict could hardly have been based on a careful study of these sermons; rather, it sprang from Schweitzer's being a great ethical philosopher. The series of sermons on the specific topic of ethics from the year 1919, in which he developed the basic principle of Reverence for Life, can be classified as ethical sermons in the strict sense of the word.

It is obvious that in a man like Albert Schweitzer, a man of deeds and achievements, everything is directed to one end—the realization of Christianity in life. This aim, to become one not only with the suffering, but more especially with the active will, of Jesus is what gives the sermons their character. But his is always primarily a religious, not a moralistic, impulse. Schweitzer's sermons lack the legalistic element that characterizes the moralistic sermon. It may be stated that Albert Schweitzer did not preach rules at all but, rather, that he preached the gospel. His words are helpful and strengthening, never threatening or judging. This can be seen from the way in which he introduces his texts. For example, in one place he says, "This promise is like a sunrise."

This is the teaching of neither the moralist or the Pharisee, nor is it the fanaticism of the preacher of repentance. He expressed his opinion of that type of sermon: "I cannot speak to you about repentance like the powerful preachers of repentance who appeared in times past. Nor would I want to. They seem to me like devastating thunderstorms pouring rain upon the earth. They do not refresh it in the way the same amount of water would have done if, instead of descending in torrents and washing away the soil, it had come down like gentle rain. John the Baptist was a powerful preacher. But by his gentle way of speaking to the people, Jesus surely achieved much more and produced much deeper repentance for sin. Whoever among us would address others on sin and repentance must do so as one sinner to another, and everything he says that is truthful is a fragment of his own experience."*

4. The language of the sermons is *very simple*. Schweitzer avoids learned phrases; at the same time he deliberately addresses simple folk without speaking down to them. He occasionally said of himself that he preached not as a theologian but as a layman. He mentioned this almost apologetically, giving as the reason for it his lack of time, especially during his medical studies. But the reasons lay deeper. For even before the period of these studies he preached in a basically similar, simple way. Rather, it was part of his charisma that he was able to express the deepest thoughts quite simply in order that listeners of the most varied intellectual levels alike might be touched.

---

* Sermon of September 21, 1912.

This simple sermon language is made extremely colorful and vivid by its wealth of comparisons and illustrations. His language is never abstract but filled to the brim with concrete illustrations. The pictures are often brief analogies full of meaning; at other times there are parables of greater length, and full of poetic beauty too, taken from the observations of daily life. They are powerful indications of the extent to which Albert Schweitzer was a man of concrete imagination and perception rather than of abstract thought. He is a close observer, and his pictures become parables. It would not be wrong to conclude that he modeled his sermons on the picturesque language of the parables of Jesus.

5. In the sermons, especially those of Advent, Christmas, and Passiontide, the pervasion of an almost mystical nearness of Jesus is noticeable. Only rarely does Schweitzer speak of Jesus in dogmatic terms. Everything is rooted deeply in a blessed experience of community of will and life with the Lord. A proximity and relationship with Jesus Christ glows through everything like a hidden fire. The impulse to action, discipleship, and sacrifice as well as his dedication to the bearing of heavy burdens all flow from the promise, "Behold, I am with you all the days." Thus Schweitzer's preaching about Jesus has factuality and a contemporary character. In this communion, our historical distance from Jesus is overcome and the same contemporary closeness is achieved, in which alone the life of faith can be perfected.

The sermons give us a more immediate glimpse of Albert Schweitzer's piety than do his published writings. Despite his outgoing mien, Schweitzer was actually shy and withdrawn. But in his sermons he allows his congregation—and now his readers—to catch a glimpse of his inmost self withheld from the public in his books. A great deal of personal confession is revealed in these sermons. They show us the unity of theology, faith, and life in this great man. What we encounter page after page, what raises us up, moves, helps, and sustains us, is the warmth of a deep Christian piety that lives in constant intimate contact with Christ. Across the decades Albert Schweitzer speaks to us straight from his heart, moving us, helping and guiding us, just as he did his parishioners at St. Nicolai's.

ULRICH NEUENSCHWANDER

Zollikofen, near Berne
March, 1966